VIEL SPAß!

PUPIL'S BOOK

Graham Sims   Gary Chambers   Dieter Hecht

HEINEMANN
EDUCATIONAL

Heinemann Educational,
a division of Heinemann Educational Books Ltd,
Halley Court, Jordan Hill, Oxford OX2 8EJ

OXFORD   LONDON   EDINBURGH
MELBOURNE SYDNEY AUCKLAND
IBADAN NAIROBI GABORONE HARARE
KINGSTON   PORTSMOUTH N H (USA)
SINGAPORE   MADRID

First published 1989
Reprinted 1989

British Library CIP Data
Sims, Graham
Viel Spaß!
Pupil's book
1. German language—Textbooks for foreign speakers—English
I. Title II. Chambers, Gary   III. Hecht, Dieter
438   PF3112
ISBN 0–435–38863–0

Designed and typeset by Oxprint Ltd, Oxford

Printed and bound in Great Britain by Butler and Tanner Ltd, Frome and London

Acknowledgements
The authors and publishers would like to thank the following
for permission to use their material:
Mary Glasgow Publications Ltd.
Ulrich P. Wienke
David Simson
Embassy of the Federal Republic of Germany
Miele
Presse-Bild-Poss
Inter Nationes

Thanks also go to:
Familie Möckel, Wuppertal
Matthias Koch, Wuppertal
Familie Römer, Köln
Familie Kaiser, Wermelskirchen
Staff and Pupils of Heisenberg Gymnasium, Gladbeck
Yvonne Ditzel, Wuppertal
Staff and Pupils of Carl Duisberg Gymnasium, Wuppertal
Staff and Pupils of Grundschule Seeberg, Köln
Kirstin Krauskopf, Köln
Ulka Petri + relatives
Yarm School, Cleveland
The Latymer School, Edmonton
It has not been possible in all cases to trace copyright holders; the publishers would be
glad to hear from any such unacknowledged copyright holders.

CONTENTS

WO WOHNST DU?

In this unit you will practise:

▷ explaining where your home town/village is,

▶ describing it and talking about the facilities it offers,

▷ expressing where you would rather live – in the town or in the country.

A. Woher kommst du?

Hör zu! ❶

We have asked six young people from German-speaking countries to tell you who they are and where they are from. Listen to their brief statements and, for each person, note down in your notebook information on as many of the following points as possible:

a) his/her name,

b) his/her age,

c) the country he/she is from,

d) the town/village he/she is from,

e) the name of the county/district in which it is situated,

f) what kind of a place it is (an industrial town, a small town, a large capital),

g) where it is situated (on the coast, in the mountains, on a lake, on a river, on an island),

h) how many people live there.

Jetzt bist du dran!

You are spending a fortnight with your German penfriend. She has invited you to come to school with her for a day. Her teacher asks you to introduce yourself to the class. What do you say? You want to tell them more than just your name, so remember to include as many points as possible from the list (a – h) under *Hör zu!* ❶ above.

Hör zu! ❷

You will now overhear four short conversations in which two people meet and talk about where they live or where they are going to live. Your teacher will stop the tape after each conversation. Make notes on the following:

a) the circumstances (What has just happened to them? What are they planning to do?),

b) the name of the town/village in which they live or are about to live,

c) the exact location of their village/town or home (in the centre of town, on the edge of town, in the mountains, on a river, on the coast, near a lake, near a border, near an airport, south/west/east/north of another town).

Eine Ansichtskarte

Your friend Claire has established contact with a German penfriend. She shows you the postcard she has just received from Helga.

> Köln, den 14. September
>
> Liebe Claire!
>
> Vielen Dank für Deinen netten Brief und das schöne Bild von Deiner Stadt. Wohnst Du gern in Slough? Wo liegt Slough ganz genau? Vielleicht komme ich nächstes Jahr mal zu Besuch!
> Wann kommst Du denn mal nach Köln? Köln ist eine große, interessante Stadt. Sie hat knapp eine Million Einwohner. Hier gibt's jede Menge zu tun.
> Schreib bald mal wieder und erzähl mir was über Slough. Bis dann, mach's gut!
> Helga

Jetzt schreibst du!

Helga's postcard has reminded you that you have forgotten to tell your penfriend that you have moved. You'd better send him/her a postcard immediately! Tell him/her what your new town or village is called, where it is situated, how big or small it is and what impression you have got of your new home so far.

B. Das Leben in der Stadt

Hör zu! ❸

A Norbert, Ilse, Dettmer, Jochen, and Silke (in this order) are now going to tell you where they live. Listen to their sentences. Then make a note in your notebook about who lives where:

a) in the industrial area,
b) in the centre of town,
c) near the old station,
d) in a suburb of the town,
e) outside the town.

1. Norbert

2. Ilse **3. Dettmer** **4. Jochen** **5. Silke**

B Listen to their statements again. Can you note down how they say in German where they live?

C When you have listened to them a third time, make a note of the advantage or disadvantage each person mentions of living where they do.

Köln – eine interessante Stadt

Der Kölner Dom

Monika, the older sister of your German penfriend, with whom you are staying, is a P.E. and German teacher. She lives in Cologne but teaches in a school near Wuppertal. She has just prepared her German lesson for the next day. She has written out some sentences about various amenities of the city of Cologne which are to assist her pupils in writing a short essay.

What are the amenities she has written about and what reason does Monika give for liking or disliking each one?

1. Wenn wir Gäste haben, gehen wir oft zum Kölner Dom. Der Dom ist das schönste Gebäude in der ganzen Stadt. Ich gehe gern hin.

2. Die Verbindungen zwischen Köln und den anderen Städten in Deutschland, und sogar in ganz Europa, sind sehr gut. Vom Hauptbahnhof kann man fast überall hinfahren.

3. Als Sportlehrerin bin ich hier sehr zufrieden. Hier sind jede Menge Hallen- und Freibäder, und es gibt auch ein großes Stadion. Man hat viele Sportmöglichkeiten.

4. In der Stadtmitte macht das Einkaufen überhaupt keinen Spaß. Die Fußgängerzone ist immer so voll! Man hat kaum Platz zum Gehen!

5. Die besten Discos und Restaurants befinden sich in der Altstadt. Leider sind aber die Preise viel zu hoch.

Hör zu! ❹

Monika's mother has invited her new neighbour round for afternoon coffee. *Frau Amberg* has just moved into the area and hopes to get some information from *Frau Pausch*. Listen carefully to their conversation. List the facilities and services which *Frau Pausch* mentions. You should be able to note down at least fifteen.

C. Das Wohnen auf dem Land

Hör zu! ❺

A Udo, Achim, Sigrid, Elke, and Peter (in this order) are going to tell you whereabouts in the country they live. Listen to their sentences. Then try to link the names to the places and note down in your notebook who lives where:

a) by a river,

b) in the mountains,   d) in the forest,

c) right by the coast,   e) on a small island.

B When you have listened to their statements again, can you note down how they say in German where they live?

C Once you have listened to them a third time, write down in English the advantages or disadvantages they mention of living where they do.

Unser Dorf – Edenbergen

Together with two friends of his, the younger brother of your German penfriend has taken part in an essay-writing competition for his school magazine. They have won a prize and their essay has been printed. Your penfriend has proudly sent you a copy. Read it carefully. Then try and answer the questions on the top of the next page.

UNSER AUFSATZWETTBEWERB!

Und hier, liebe Leser, sind die Gewinner unseres Wettbewerbs, in dem Schüler über ihren Wohnort berichteten. Der erste Preis und damit drei Eintrittskarten für das Konzert von Nina Hagen geht an Stefan Kienle, Marcus Engel und Rainald Haak aus der 7. Klasse unserer Realschule. Lest selbst:

„Wir wohnen in einem Dorf namens Edenbergen; es liegt nicht weit von der Stadt Augsburg entfernt. Die Busverbindungen von unserem Dorf in die nähere Umgebung sind recht gut. In unserem Wohnort gibt es einen kleinen Laden. Dort kann man alles kaufen, was man so braucht. Zum Fußballspielen haben wir einen schönen Sportplatz. Für die Kleinen gibt es auch einen Spielplatz mit allen möglichen Geräten. Im Dorf gibt es eine Gastwirtschaft, in der man sehr gut essen kann. Die meisten Häuser im Dorf sind Bauernhöfe. Wenn es schneit, können wir Skifahren und rodeln, denn bei uns gibt es einen etwa 350 Meter hohen Berg. Wir haben auch ein Feuerwehrhaus im Dorf und eine freiwillige Feuerwehr. Eine Kirche haben wir nicht im Dorf. Darum gehen wir nach Batsenhofen, das ist etwa einen Kilometer von Edenbergen entfernt, zum Gottesdienst. Unser Dorf gefällt uns gut. Wir können Fußball spielen und auf den ruhigen Straßen ohne Gefahr radfahren."

Kapiert?

1. Where is the village of Edenbergen situated?
2. What is the public transport service like to the surrounding villages?
3. Name four sorts of building you would find in Edenbergen.
4. Name four activities you could do in Edenbergen.
5. Do the boys like living in their village?
6. What two advantages of living in a village are mentioned in the last sentence of the essay?

Jetzt schreibst du!

Stefan's essay has reminded you that you have not yet told your penfriend much about where you live. Write a letter to him/her in German telling him/her about the town or village in which you live. Greet your friend and thank him/her for his/her letter. Tell him/her about the facilities in your town or village – shops, sporting facilities, museums, entertainment. Say whether you like living there and how you spend your time. Finish the letter hoping he/she will write again soon. Below you will find some characteristics of the town and country to help you with this exercise.

D. Stadt oder Land?

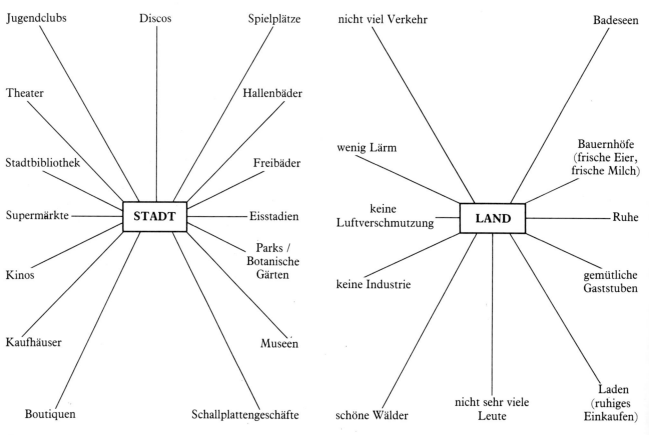

This is how you say in German where you prefer to live:

Ich wohne **lieber**	in der Stadt	**als**	auf dem Land.
	auf dem Land		in der Stadt.

Ich finde es	in der Stadt	**besser**	**als**	auf dem Land.
	auf dem Land	**schöner**		in der Stadt.
		ruhiger		
		sauberer		

Ich ziehe es vor,	in der Stadt	**zu** wohnen.
	auf dem Land	

This is how you argue your point:

, weil da/dort/hier .... ist/sind.
, weil es hier mehr .... gibt als ....
, weil es hier weniger .... gibt als ....

Jetzt bist du dran!

Conduct a small survey amongst your classmates. Include the following questions in your questionnaire:

1. Wo wohnst du?
2. Gefällt es dir dort?
3. Warum oder warum nicht?
4. Möchtest du lieber woanders wohnen?
5. Wenn ja, wo und warum?

Here are some more detailed questions you might wish to ask your classmates:

6. Was für Einkaufsmöglichkeiten gibt es in deinem Wohnort?
7. Was für Freizeitsmöglichkeiten gibt es?
8. Gibt es viele Sehenswürdigkeiten?

ZU HAUSE

In this unit you will practise:

▷ talking about your family,

▶ describing people,

▷ describing your house or flat,

▶ talking about the furniture,

▷ describing your own room.

A. Die Familie

Hör zu! ❶

We asked Rolf, Ayse, Jutta, Bernd, Sören, and Gudrun to tell you about their families. Listen to what they say. Whenever your teacher stops the tape, write down as many details as possible about the members of their family which each one of them has mentioned, for example:

> Rolf: Has got ... brother(s)/sister(s).
> His/her name is ...
> His/her age is ...
> He/she has ... hair (long, short, curly, wavy, silky, straight, thick, thin, brown, black, etc.).
> He/she is . . . (nice, nasty, bad-tempered, quiet, shy, cheeky, sweet, good-natured, etc.)
> He/she has a ... face.
> He/she has ... eyes. (brown, green, blue, grey, etc.)
> He/she is ... metre and ...centimetres tall.
> He/she is ... than ... (younger, older).
> He/she is a ... (pupil, student, working as a ...).

Jetzt bist du dran!

Your exchange student from Germany has just arrived. Your parents are interested in learning a little more about his/her family. As they do not speak any German, you have to do the asking. Ask questions such as:

1. Hast du Geschwister?
2. Hast du einen Bruder/eine Schwester?
3. Wie alt ist dein Bruder/deine Schwester?
4. Was für Haar hat er/sie?
5. Welche Augenfarbe hat er/sie?

6. Wie groß ist er/sie?

7. Wie alt ist er/sie?

8. Wie heißt er/sie?

9. Geht er/sie noch zur Schule?

10. Was macht er/sie?

11. Wie heißt deine Tante/dein Onkel?

12. Wie alt ist deine Großmutter/dein Großvater?

13. Wohnt er/sie bei euch im Haus?

Ein Familienfoto

A classmate of yours, who isn't very good at German, has received this letter and photo from a new penfriend. Can you help by explaining what Sabine says in her letter?

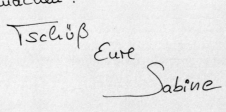

Hallo!

Ich heiße Sabine und wenn Ihr auf das Bild schaut, seht Ihr mich in der Mitte.

Auf der rechten Seite sitzt mein Vater, sein Name ist Gerd. Er arbeitet mit meiner Mutter zusammen in der Textilbranche. Meine Mutter heißt Gudrun und sitzt auf dem Bild links neben mir.

Ich bin 18 Jahre alt und gehe noch zur Schule. Im Frühling 1987 werde ich mein Abitur machen, und danach möchte ich studieren.

Was ich studieren möchte, weiß ich noch nicht genau; voraussichtlich Journalismus, aber bis dahin ist noch viel Zeit.

So, nun muß ich leider Schluß machen.

Tschüß

Eure

Sabine

Ein Familienstammbaum

You are interested in family history and you have just compiled your family tree. Your German friend Jörg has asked you to do the same for him. He has written down some information about his family for you. When you have read his description, draw up a family tree for him. Give the names of the various members of his family and any information as to their age, whether they are still living, etc.

Ich lebe zusammen mit meiner Mutter in einer Wohnung in einem Mehrfamilienhaus. Dort wohne ich seit meiner Geburt. Mein Vater Josef lebt seit acht Jahren nicht mehr. Mit fünfzehn Jahren bin ich der Jüngste bei uns zu Hause. In unserem Haus lebt auch mein 18 jähriger Bruder. Er heißt Uwe. Ich habe noch einen Bruder, der mit seiner Frau und seinen drei Söhnen in einem anderen Stadtteil Osnabrücks wohnt. Er ist 28 Jahre, seine Frau 26. Er heißt Norbert, und meine Schwägerin Monika. Meine drei Neffen heißen Jens, Carsten und Benjamin. Sie sind acht, vier und zwei Jahre alt.

Jetzt bist du dran!

Your penfriend Susanne has asked some friends over for afternoon coffee. You have just been looking through an old photograph album of hers which contains lots of pictures of her and her family. You happen to have a photograph of your family on you (bring one in to school!) and show it to Susanne and her friends. Work in groups of four to five pupils each and take it in turns to explain your picture. Say something about each person in it, for example: the name, age, occupation, family relationship, hobbies, etc.

Jetzt schreibst du!

Send a photograph in which your entire family appears to Susanne's older brother Walter whom you met on your previous visit and who is also a good friend of yours. Describe to him who is who in your photograph and tell him a little bit about each person.

Hör zu! ❷

In the course of the coffee afternoon, Susanne, Klaus, Jan and Elke (in this order) talk about some people they know. Listen carefully to what they say. Whenever your teacher stops the tape, write down the correct characteristic mentioned for each person talked about. Here is a choice of answers. Pick out the correct one!

a) Susanne's sister Angelika: spoiled, hard-working, lazy.

b) Klaus's friend Andrea: intelligent, stupid, impatient.

c) Jan's nephew: honest, cheeky, shy.

d) Elke's aunt: energetic, pessimistic, old-fashioned.

e) Maths teacher: humorous, imaginative, strict.

Meine Familie

Gisela, a schoolfriend of Susanne's, has come to see you. She has written a letter to her English penfriend in which she tells him about her family. She wants you to help her translate it into English. Read the letter and then translate the key points.

Bochum, den 14. Juni

Lieber Gerald,

Vielen Dank für Deinen lieben Brief. Du hast ja eine ganz schön große Familie. Ich schreib Dir heute etwas über meine Familie.

Mein Vater heißt Gerald, genau wie Du! Er ist groß, schlank und grauhaarig. Er liest gern und ist überhaupt sehr ruhig. Was ich besonders an ihm mag ist, daß er immer so verständnisvoll ist. Ich kann mit allen meinen Problemen zu ihm kommen. Leider ist er abends nach der Arbeit oft müde.

Meine Mutter Martha ist neun Jahre jünger als mein Vater. Sie ist sehr jugendlich und sportlich und sehr modisch. Wir beide haben fast die gleiche Kleidergröße. Das finde ich toll. Wir tauschen immer unsere Klamotten untereinander aus. Sie ist allerdings rothaarig. Da passen natürlich nicht alle meine Sachen zu ihr.

Ich habe einen Bruder. Er heißt Martin, ist vierzehn Jahre alt und sehr gutaussehend. Martin ist, wie ich, sehr lebhaft und sportlich. Er geht jeden Tag schwimmen und spielt auch in einem Fußballverein. Er ist auch ungeheuer strebsam. Er will später einmal Computer-Operator werden. Er sitzt jeden Tag vor seinem Heimcomputer.

So, nun kannst Du Dir ein Bild von uns machen. Was treibst Du denn so in Worthing? Schreib doch mal. Bis bald, es grüßt Dich

Gisela

Kapiert?

Have you understood everything? Pick out of this list the qualities which apply to Gisela's family.

Father: a) very fat; b) bald; c) understanding; d) grey-haired;
e) lively; f) energetic; g) quiet; h) tired; i) tall; j) bad-tempered.

Mother: a) older than father; b) boring; c) intelligent;
d) fashionable; e) inactive; f) red-haired; g) impatient;
h) old-fashioned; i) youthful; j) sporty.

Martin: a) ambitious; b) lazy; c) quiet; d) energetic; e) lively;
f) a swimmer; g) dull; h) good-looking; i) a stamp collector; j) a football player.

Jetzt schreibst du!

Write a letter to your German penfriend and tell him/her about your family. You could use Gisela's letter to help you.

Die Familie Ambruster

This is the *Familienstammbaum*, the family tree of the Ambruster family from Hamburg. It gives you details about the circumstances of each member of the family. Read it carefully, then answer the questions on the top of the next page.

Herr und Frau Ambruster
verheiratet – 32 Jahre
Wohnort – Hamburg
4 Kinder

Helga
Alter – 24
verlobt mit Kurt – 2 Monate,
Heiraten nächstes Jahr
Lehrerin
Kurt – Student

Karl
Alter – 26
Getrennt – 2 Jahre
Wohnort – Bremen
Wohnt mit Freundin
Arbeitslos

Josef
Alter – 29
Verheiratet – 3 Jahre
Frau - Ingrid
1 Kind - Hans - 6 Monate
Wohnort - Dortmund

Bärbel
Alter – 22
Geschieden – 1 Jahr
Wohnort – Hamburg
Briefträgerin

Kapiert?

1. How many children do Mr and Mrs Ambruster have?
2. How long have they been married?
3. What is Josef Ambruster's son called?
4. How long has Karl Ambruster been separated?
5. What is Helga Ambruster's job?
6. Does Karl live on his own?
7. Is Bärbel Ambruster married?
8. Where does Josef Ambruster live?
9. Is he single?
10. What does Bärbel do for a living?

Jetzt schreibst du!

Write a detailed account of the Ambruster family in German. The family tree will give you all the details you need.

B. Das Haus

Hör zu! ❸

You are sitting in on the German class of your friend Martin in Germany. The teacher asks eight pupils to tell the class where they live and what their home is like. Listen to what they say. Whenever your teacher stops the tape, write down as much information about each person's home as you can. Concentrate on points such as:

a) what type of building it is,
b) whether it is a house or a flat,
c) details about the area,
d) the number of rooms,
e) whether there is a garden, a garage, a patio or a balcony,
f) whether it is quiet or noisy there,
g) whether they like living where they do.

Jetzt schreibst du!

Michaela has written you a letter in which she tells you about her home. Read it carefully. Write a reply in which you explain where you live, with whom you live, where your house/flat is, whether you like living there, etc.

Hallo!

Vielen Dank für Deine Postkarte aus Spanien. Sie ist erst heute bei mir angekommen, da wir eine neue Adresse haben. Es freut mich, daß Du einen schönen Urlaub gehabt hast.

Leider konnten wir dieses Jahr nicht wegfahren, da der Umzug vor drei Wochen viel Geld gekostet hat. Wir wohnen jetzt in einem vierstöckigen Haus in einem Vorort von Essen. Unsere Wohnung liegt im 3. Stock. Sie ist ganz schön. Wir haben 4 Zimmer und Küche, Diele, Bad und Balkon. Aber es gefällt mir hier nicht sehr. Wir wohnen direkt an der Hauptstraße. Da ist immer so viel Verkehr, und man kann nirgendwo spielen. Zur Schule muß ich jetzt mit dem Bus fahren, auch wenn ich nur eben in die Stadt will. Außerdem wohnen hier im Haus fast nur alte Leute, und ich habe noch keine Freunde im Haus.

In was für einer Wohnung wohnst Du eigentlich? Oder habt Ihr ein Haus? Hast Du gute Nachbarn und Spielkameraden? Liegt Euer Haus in der Stadtmitte oder in einem Vorort? Schreib mir doch und erzähle.
Deine Michaela

C. Die Zimmer

Hör zu! ❹

You have just arrived at your host family's flat for your exchange visit. Lydia is showing you round the place explaining where things are. Listen carefully to what she says. Fill in the plan on the worksheet which your teacher has given you. (Worksheet A of this unit). You will find a jumbled list of the rooms mentioned beneath the plan, which will help you. Give the English equivalents of the rooms as well.

Jetzt bist du dran!

Draw the ground plan of your own house or flat. Label all the rooms and explain the plan to your partner. Give him/her a guided tour round your house or flat!

Jetzt schreibst du!

Write a letter to your penfriend describing your house or flat. Say in what sort of house you live or in what kind of house your flat is. Say whether there is a garage, a garden, a patio, a balcony, etc. Mention the number of rooms you have and say what they are called. End the letter by asking your penfriend a few questions about his/her house.

Immobilien-Inserate

Look at the advertisements for houses and flats below and read them carefully.

1. **Hangelar** EF-Reihenhaus, 5 Zimmer, Garage, 133 m² Wfl. ausbaufähig, v. Privat. DM 350.000,-Angebote an Gen.-Anz., Bonn, Am Martinsplatz, unter BZ 99 795.

2. **DO, Kl. Kielstraße 5**
   2-Zi.-Komf.-Wohnung
   mit Bad. Balkon. Nachtspeicher-heizung ab sof. zu vermieten. Mietpr. inkl. Nebenk. 390.- DM. Garage (Mietpreis 45.- DM) kann ebenfalls angemietet werden. Telefon 02 31-81 04 25

3. **Appartement**, voll möbliert, 35 m² Wohn/Schlafraum (Wohnwand mit integriertem Schrankbett, Teppich-boden), Komplettküche, Du-sche-WC, Flur, Abstellraum, Gar-tenbenutzung, Telefon, Kabel-TV, ruhige Lage, Buslinien 25, 35, 36, Haltestelle Rehsprung/Holzlar, zum 1. 9., Miete 400,- u. NK 70,-. Ruf 48 13 34.

4. **Möbl. Zimmer**, DO-Wambel, Miete DM 180 + NK, Gemeinschaftsbad, 2. OG, ab sofort zu verm. Heinz Fiersbach Hausverwaltungen GmbH, Saarlandstr. 79, Dortmund 1, ☎ 02 31-12 33 71 oder 10 38 36.

5. **Nöthen Massivhaus**
   Wir planen und bauen für Sie Ihr Eigenheim schlüssel., in massiver Bauweise auf Ihrem oder einem von uns vermittelten Grundstück.
   Unser Architektenteam berät Sie kostenlos.

   Z.B. Haus Detmold, inkl. Keller und Garage, 109 m² Wohnfläche
   230.000,- DM
   als Ausbauhaus
   199.000,- DM
   Nöthen Wohnbau
   BONN-RÖTTGEN
   Tel.: (02 28) 25 10 11 (Mo.-Fr.)
   Sa./So. (0 22 26) 1 37 27

6.
   Direkt an der Stemmerwiese...
   finden Sie so **exquisite Grundrisse** wie z.B. den Woh-nungstyp „Orangenbaum" (4 Zimmer, 84 m², als Alternative mit „Schwedenküche").

   Die Auswahl ist noch groß:
   2-Zimmer-Whg., 54 bis 65 m², ab DM 239.900,-
   3-Zimmer-Whg. 74 bis 89 m², ab DM 309.900,-
   4-Zimmer-Whg. 88 m², DM 336.100,-
   Erdgeschoß-Whgn. mit eigenem Gartenanteil
   Einige schicke Dachwohnungen.
   GARTENHOF SENDLINGER BERG
   Eigentumswohnungen an der Stemmerwiese/Winkstraße

   BERATUNG*
   für alle Baywobau-Objekte
   am Baugrundstück Winkstraße
   Sa. + So. 29./30.12. jeweils 13 – 16 Uhr
   und am Neujahrstag 1.1.85 13 – 16 Uhr
   Mittwoch 15.30 – 19 Uhr

   Baywobau
   Baywobau Baubetreuung GmbH · 8 Mü. 80 · Prinzregentenplatz 17

Decide to which advertisement each of the following people should reply:

a) A business friend of your father who wants to rent a furnished flat with a garden. He is quite well-off and not too worried about the cost.

b) A friend of your older sister who wishes to rent a small flat immediately, preferably with a garage.

c) Your penfriend's sister who is a student. She is looking for a furnished room for not more than DM 200 a month.

d) Friends of your host family, a young couple, who wish to buy a terraced house with a garage.

e) Three friends who are looking for a large flat to share. They would like it to be in the southern part of the inner city in a quiet situation.

7. **Maisonettwohnung**, südl. Innen-stadt, ruhige Lage, 3 - 4 Schlafz., 1 Wohnraum, KDB, Balkon, Neuaus-bau, erstkl. Ausst., Teppichboden, Isoliervergl., eigene Gaszentralhei-zung, ☎ 02 31-54 04 21 5.

Hör zu! ❺

A We have asked five young German people to talk about their rooms. Listen to what they say. Whenever your teacher stops the tape, turn to the grid on worksheet B of this unit and tick the items which are mentioned by each speaker.

B Listen again. Make a note of any extra contents of the rooms, such as posters, pictures, flags, stereos, etc.

Jetzt bist du dran!

Here is a selection of photographs showing different rooms. Describe in German what kind of rooms they are and what they have in them.

1.
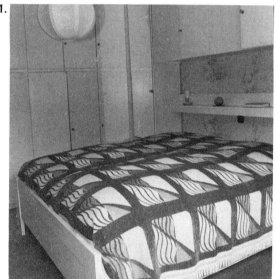

2.

3.

4.

Mein Reich

This is a letter Bärbel has written to her English penfriend Helen. Read it carefully. Draw Bärbel's room and label all the items it contains in German.

Vokabeln

das stinkt mir – I do not like it much
urgemütlich – very cosy
die Kommode – chest of drawers
vermachen – (slang) to give to
die Unterwäsche – underwear
der Pulli – pullover
der Aufkleber – sticker
das sieht irre aus – (slang) that looks fantastic
die Lümmelecke – (slang) a cosy little corner
die Truhe – chest
irgendwie – somehow
halt die Ohren steif – (slang) keep your chin up

Neustadt, den 25. August

Liebe Helen,

Heute will ich Dir mal beschreiben, wie mein Zimmer aussieht. Dann kannst Du Dir ein Bild davon machen, wo ich immer sitze und Briefe an Dich schreibe. Also, mein Zimmer ist nicht sehr groß. Es ist das kleinste von den drei Schlafzimmern in unserer Wohnung. Das größte Schlafzimmer haben meine Eltern, und im zweitgrößten schläft meine Schwester. Das stinkt mir etwas, daß sie ein größeres Zimmer hat, bloß weil sie älter ist als ich!

Aber Du, mein Zimmer ist urgemütlich! Hinten an der Wand steht mein Bett und daneben ein kleines Tischchen mit einer Leselampe. Ich lese nämlich furchtbar gern im Bett! In einer Ecke steht eine schöne alte Kommode. Die hat mir meine Oma mal vermacht. Ich habe darin Kleidungsstücke wie Unterwäsche, Socken, Pullis und Sportzeug untergebracht. Rechts an der Wand steht mein Kleiderschrank. Der nimmt ganz schön viel Platz weg. Damit er nicht so langweilig aussieht, habe ich ihn mit lauter bunten Aufklebern beklebt. Das sieht irre aus, sage ich Dir! Eine kleine Lümmelecke habe ich natürlich auch. Ich hab einfach ein paar große Sitzkissen auf die Erde gelegt und ein kleines Tischchen aus einer alten Truhe gemacht. Da sitze ich nun also und schreibe diesen Brief. Leider ist mein Zimmer nie besonders aufgeräumt. Irgendwie brauche ich einfach ein bißchen Unordnung um mich rum. Schreib mir doch mal, wie Dein Zimmer aussieht, ja?

Deine Bärbel

Jetzt schreibst du!

Reply to Bärbel's letter. Describe to her what your room looks like. Alternatively, you could describe any other room in your house or flat.

DER ALLTAG

In this unit you will practise:

▷ explaining what you do during the day,

▶ explaining what you do in the evening,

▷ talking about your way to school,

▶ explaining how you help around the house,

▷ talking about your pets,

▶ describing what you do at weekends,

▷ talking about pocket money and how you spend it.

A. Wann machst du denn das?

Hör zu! ❶

You will hear seven short dialogues which relate to a particular time of day. Listen to what the people say and, whenever your teacher stops the tape, write down what time of day is mentioned:

a) Uli,   c) Renate,   e) Die beiden Arbeitskollegen,   g) Monika.

b) Udo,   d) Claudia,   f) Heidis Vater,

Wann machst du das?

Look at these pictures which each show an activity most people carry out every day. Read phrases a – l below and match the correct phrase to the right picture.

a) Ich gehe einkaufen.

b) Ich sehe fern.

c) Ich räume mein Zimmer auf.

d) Ich gehe mit dem Hund spazieren.

e) Ich kämme mich.

f) Ich lese die Zeitung.

g) Ich trockne ab.

h) Ich mache meine Hausaufgaben.

i) Ich schminke mich.

j) Ich höre Schallplatten.

k) Ich wasche mich.

l) Ich putze mir die Zähne.

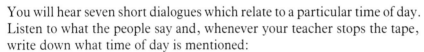

Jetzt bist du dran!

Use the pictures 1 to 12 to ask your partner questions about when he/she does a particular thing every day. Ask, for example:

1. Wann stehst du auf?
2. Wann gehst du ins Bett?
3. Wann gehst du mit deinem Hund spazieren?
4. Wann wäschst du dich?
5. Wann duschst du?
6. Wann gehst du einkaufen?
7. Wann schminkst du dich?
8. Wann putzt du dir die Zähne?
9. Wann hörst du Schallplatten?
   usw.

Mein Tageslauf

Read Kemal and Daniela's accounts of a normal school day. Draw a grid into your notebook. In three columns side by side write down how each pupil spends the day. Write down the time in the left-hand column. Give as much detail as you can.

Kemal:

„Ich stehe jeden Tag um 6.20 Uhr auf und ziehe mich an. Danach gehe ich ins Bad, putze mir die Zähne und wasche mich. Dann frühstücke ich und packe meine Schulsachen zusammen. Um etwa 7.10 Uhr gehe ich schön langsam zur Bushaltestelle. Im Bus treffe ich meine Klassenkameraden. Nach einer halben Stunde kommen wir dann in Augsburg an. Bis zur Realschule müssen wir noch ein Stück laufen. Um 8.00 Uhr beginnen die ersten drei Schulstunden. Jede Stunde dauert fünfundvierzig Minuten. Um 10.15 Uhr haben wir dann Pause. Beim Gongschlag gehen wir in unsere Klassenzimmer zurück. Dann haben wir meistens noch bis um 12.50 Uhr Unterricht. Um 13.30 Uhr komme ich nach Hause. Nachdem ich etwas gegessen habe, mache ich meine Hausaufgaben. Das dauert so zwei bis drei Stunden. Wenn ich mit den Schularbeiten fertig bin, gehe ich meistens zu Freunden. Wir spielen zusammen oder unterhalten uns."

Daniela:

„Ich stehe meistens um 6.50 Uhr auf. Wenn ich mich angezogen habe, gehe ich frühstücken. Um 7.20 Uhr verlasse ich das Haus und mache mich auf den Schulweg. Ich brauche mit dem Velo nur fünf Minuten bis zur Schule. Von 7.25 Uhr bis 9.55 Uhr habe ich drei Stunden. Danach haben wir eine Viertelstunde Pause. Dann haben wir nochmal zwei Stunden, und um 11.50 Uhr kehren wir nach Hause zurück. Nach dem Essen mache ich die Küche sauber. Wenn mir noch Zeit übrig bleibt, mache ich noch Hausaufgaben. Um 13.30 Uhr gehe ich wieder zur Schule, wo wir noch weitere drei Stunden haben. Gleich nach der Schule habe ich entweder Klavierstunde, oder ich gehe in die Turnhalle, wo wir Mädchenriege haben. Ab und zu gehe ich auch nach Hause, um meine Hausaufgaben zu machen."

Kemal

Vokabeln

die Mädchenriege –
girls' team/squad
Velo = Fahrrad (Schweiz)

Daniela

Hör zu! ❷

Listen to this German pupil's description of a normal school day twice. Whenever your teacher stops the tape, write down as much detail as you can about what is being done at what time. You could either fill in a section of your worksheet (A) or draw a grid like the one for the previous exercise in your notebook.

Und was ist am Abend?

Read what Lisa and Florian usually do in the evenings. Make a grid in your notebook and write down what they do at what time.

Lisa:

„Den Abend verbringe ich entweder mit Freunden oder mit meiner Familie, ab und zu gehe ich auch schwimmen oder Squash spielen. Und wenn ich abends fernsehe, stricke oder bastle ich nebenbei ganz gerne. Meist endet mein Tag um 10.30 Uhr, wenn ich ins Bett gehe, manchmal lese ich jedoch noch ein oder zwei Stunden. Spätestens um 12.00 Uhr mache ich mein Licht aus."

Lisa

Florian:

„Wenn ich mit meinen Hausaufgaben fertig bin, gehe ich ins nahegelegene Jugendzentrum, wo ich meist Karten oder Tischtennis spiele. Um 21.00 Uhr schließt das Jugendzentrum, und meine Freunde und ich gehen noch zu einem von uns nach Hause oder ins Eiscafé, um einen Kaffee zu trinken oder ein Eis zu essen. Meistens gehe ich so gegen 22 Uhr heim. Manchmal sehe ich dann noch ein wenig fern, und wenn nichts Besonderes mehr läuft, gehe ich schlafen."

Florian

Jetzt schreibst du!

Turn to worksheet A of this chapter. Write down in one section of it what you normally do during the day. Then ask your partner what he/she does on a normal day, for example:

Was machst du morgens/mittags/nachmittags/abends?

Write down his/her answers in a different section of your worksheet. Now he/she asks you the same questions and notes down your answers. Compare your notes at the end and see whether you have understood each other.

B. Der Schulweg

Hör zu! ❸

Your friend Max, who is attending the *Sekundarschule* at *Chorweiler*, has asked five of his classmates to tell you how they travel to school every day. Listen to what they reply. Write down in your notebook how each speaker travels to school. Be careful, some people use more than one means of transport to get there!

Jetzt bist du dran!

Work with your partner. One of you assumes the role of a German visitor who is interested in how you get to school. He/she asks you the questions below. Change roles when you have acted out the situation once.

1. Wie weit wohnst du von der Schule entfernt?
2. Wie kommst du zur Schule?
3. Wie lange brauchst du, um in die Schule zu gehen?
4. Gehst du immer den selben Weg zur Schule?
5. Und wie kommst du zur Schule, wenn es regnet oder wenn es schneit?

Jetzt schreibst du!

Conduct a survey in your classroom about how your classmates travel to school. For each person you ask, make a note in German of the type(s) of transport used and the length of the journey(s) involved. Find out who has the longest or the most complicated journey to school.

C. Das Leben zu Hause

Hör zu! ❹

You will hear ten short sentences which each mention a household chore. Look at the pictures below:

A Find the right picture for each sentence you hear and write down the relevant number in your notebook.

B Match the right caption with the right picture.

a) abwaschen
b) Briefe einwerfen
c) den Tisch decken
d) staubsaugen
e) abtrocknen
f) die Wäsche aufhängen
g) das Bad saubermachen
h) den Rasen mähen
i) mit dem Hund spazierengehen
j) das Bett machen

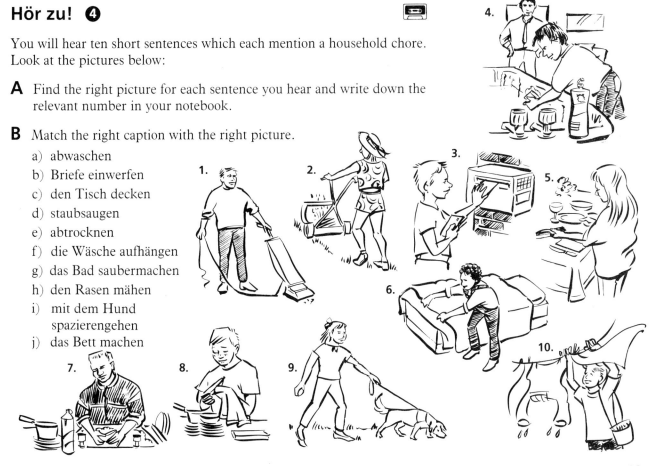

Hör zu! ❺

You will hear five short conversations in which someone is asked to help around the house. Before you listen, copy this grid into your notebook. After each conversation, fill in the details in the grid.

	Job	Response	Excuse if response is negative
Hartmut:			
Richard:			
Andreas:			
Sabine:			
Dieter:			

Jetzt bist du dran!

Your exchange partner has been staying with you for quite a while. So you think it is time for him/her to help you with the household chores. With the aid of the expressions and the vocabulary below, ask him/her (your partner will take this role) to help you. Think of as many activities as possible. If you go back to the beginning of this section (page 23), you can remind yourself of the kind of things that need doing around the house.

Change roles. Now your partner asks you for help.

Request

Könntest du mir helfen, Hast du Zeit,	den Rasen zu mähen? das Auto zu waschen? staubzusaugen? die Wäsche aufzuhängen?
Möchtest du vielleicht Kannst du bitte Würdest du bitte	den Hund ausführen? das Bad saubermachen? den Tisch decken? abtrocknen?

+ Positive Response +

Ja, gern. Ja, natürlich. Selbstverständlich, kein Problem.	Ja, sofort. Aber klar.

− Negative Response −   plus Excuse

Tut mir leid. Nein, das geht leider nicht. Nein. Warum denn ich? Was, ich? Mach das doch selber! (*rude!*)	Ich habe keine Zeit. Ich habe zu tun. Dazu habe ich keine Lust. Ich mache gerade meine Hausauf- gaben. Das ist nichts für mich. Ich bin beschäftigt.

Jetzt schreibst du!

On the basis of what you have just learned, write a short essay in German about the work you do at home, when you do it, whether you like it, etc.

D. Haustiere

Was ist denn das?

Look at these pictures and find the right animal name for each one from the list of pets below.

Animals:
a) das Meerschweinchen
b) der Goldfisch
c) der Hamster
d) das Pferd
e) der Hund
f) der Wellensittich
g) die Schildkröte
h) die Katze
i) das Kaninchen
j) der Igel
k) der Papagei

Hör zu! ❻

Some young people will tell you about their pets. Copy the grid below into your notebook. Whenever your teacher stops the tape, fill in the relevant details in the grid for each speaker.

	Type of pet	How long have they had it?	What food does it eat?
1. 2. 3. 4. 5. 6. 7.			

Jetzt bist du dran!

Interview your partner about his/her pets. Ask him/her:

a) whether he/she has got a pet (*ein Haustier*),
b) what it is called (*wie es heißt, wie er/sie es nennt*),
c) how long he/she has had it,
d) what it looks like (*wie es aussieht*),
e) whether he/she would like to have any other pets (*noch andere Haustiere*),
f) what he/she does with it (*machen mit*),
g) how often he/she feeds it (*füttern*),
h) what it eats (*fressen*),
i) where it sleeps (*schlafen*), etc.

E. Das Wochenende

Hör zu! ❼

During your exchange visit to Germany, you hear the following eight interviews in a school radio broadcast about weekend activities. Whenever your teacher stops the tape, write down what Wilfried, Alexandra, Jan, Sandra, Hartmut, Gerhard, Melanie and Gudrun usually do at weekends.

Jetzt bist du dran!

A Conduct this roleplay with your partner. One of you assumes the role of Rolf and the other that of Rainer. Rainer's role is slightly more complicated, because he has to construct his reply on the basis of the prompts given.

Rolf: Was hast du denn am Wochenende gemacht?
Rainer: Nothing special – Saturday morning – weather awful – stayed at home.
Rolf: Bist du den ganzen Tag zu Hause geblieben?
Rainer: No – read newspaper – wrote letter – went to post office.
Rolf: Am Nachmittag bin ich zum Bundesligaspiel zwischen dem 1.FC Köln und dem FC Bayern München gegangen. Warum bist du nicht mitgekommen?
Rainer: Not interested in football – met Ingrid at post office – went to her house for afternoon – listened to records.
Rolf: Das Spiel war toll! 4 : 2 für den 1. FC. Am Abend bin ich mit Jutta zum Jugendklub gegangen. Da war eine Disko.
Rainer: Evening at birthday party – lots to eat and drink.
Rolf: War am Sonntag was los?
Rainer: Church in morning – lunch at grandmother's.
Rolf: Ich habe mich endlich mal richtig ausgeschlafen. Ich bin erst

um 11.00 Uhr aufgestanden. Nachher mußte ich für meine
Englischarbeit pauken.

Rainer: Whole evening doing homework – no time to watch TV.

B Once you feel confident and have tried both roles, talk to your partner in German, without looking at the roleplay, about your last weekend.

Post von Uwe!

Read what Uwe tells Stuart about his weekend activities.

Gelsenkirchen, den 27. September

Lieber Stuart,

Herzlichen Dank für Deinen langen Brief, den ich heute endlich beantworten will. Du möchtest gern wissen, was ich so am Wochenende treibe. Nun, ich beschreibe Dir einmal, was ich an diesem Wochenende gemacht habe.

Am Samstag habe ich mich erst einmal richtig ausgeschlafen, da wir keine Schule hatten. Um 10 Uhr habe ich erst gefrühstückt! Dann bin ich mit meiner Mutter zum Einkaufen in die Stadt gefahren.

Nach dem Mittagessen bin ich zum Hallenbad gefahren. Ich schwimme nämlich furchtbar gern. Am besten bin ich im Brustschwimmen, aber kraulen kann ich auch ganz gut.

Abends bin ich dann noch zu Friedhelm gegangen. Wir wollten eigentlich Tischtennis spielen, aber dann ist Heinz, sein Bruder, gekommen und wir haben Skat gespielt, allerdings nicht um Geld. Das war auch gut so, denn ich hatte den ganzen Abend schlechte Karten und habe immer verloren.

Am Sonntag bin ich früh aufgestanden und in die Hohe Mark gefahren. Das ist ein Naturschutzgebiet nördlich vom Ruhrgebiet. Zuerst sind wir zum Segelflugplatz in die Borkenberge gefahren. Gott sei Dank war Flugtag, und ich durfte einen Rundflug im Segelflugzeug machen. Das war wirklich toll.

Auf dem Rückweg haben wir etwas Kuchen gekauft und sind zu meiner Oma zum Kaffee gefahren. Die hat sich so über unseren Besuch gefreut!

Das wär's für heute. Halt die Ohren steif.

Tschüß, Dein
Uwe

Kapiert?

Your brother asks you the following questions about Uwe's letter. Can you tell him what he wants to know?

1. Did Uwe go to school on Saturday?
2. At what time did he get up?
3. What did he do in the morning?
4. What did he do after lunch?
5. What did he do on Saturday evening?
6. Did he go anywhere on Sunday?
7. Did anything special happen?
8. What did he do at teatime?

Jetzt schreibst du!

Write a letter to your penfriend.

Tell him/her:
a) what you did on Saturday,
b) what the weather was like,
c) what you did on Sunday.

Ask him/her if he/she:
d) does the same every weekend,
e) does the same things you do at weekends.

Ask him/her to write back soon.

F. Taschengeld

Hör zu! ❽

A On German school radio, you listen to interviews with young people about pocket money. Listen carefully. Whenever your teacher stops the tape, write down:
  a) whether the speaker receives pocket money, and
  b) mention at least one item on which he/she spends it.

B When you have listened a second time, write down whether the speaker works for his/her pocket money and if so, what kind of job he/she does.

Jetzt bist du dran!

Wann bekommst du dein Taschengeld?

Ich bekomme mein Taschengeld	am Anfang der Woche. am Wochenende. einmal im Monat. jeden Freitag. am Anfang des Monats.
Ich bekomme gar nichts!	

Was mußt du dafür machen?

Ich muß	abwaschen. abtrocknen. mit dem Hund spazierengehen. einkaufen. den Rasen mähen. staubsaugen. Zeitungen austragen. das Auto waschen.
Ich brauche nichts dafür zu machen.	

Was kaufst du dir davon? Wie gibst du dein Geld aus?

Ich kaufe mir von meinem Taschengeld	Kleidung. Bücher. Süßigkeiten. Getränke. Schallplatten. Schreibwaren. Zeitschriften. Comics.	
Ich gebe mein Taschengeld für	den Jugendklub das Kino Geschenke Fahrgeld das Schwimmbad mein Mofa Sport Hobbys die Disko	aus.
Ich spare mein Taschengeld.		

On the basis of the examples given above, interview your partner and ask:

a) when he/she receives his/her pocket money,

b) what he/she has to do for it,

c) whether he/she earns pocket money with a job,

d) what he/she spends his/her pocket money on.

Once you have been through the questions once, change roles.

WIR FEIERN

In this unit you will practise:
▷ how to accept and decline invitations,
▶ what to say when you meet someone for the first time,
▷ how to introduce people,

You will find out:
▷ how Christmas is celebrated in Germany,
▶ a little about German weddings.

A. **Wir sind eingeladen**

Hör zu! ❶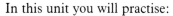

A You will listen in on five short conversations in which somebody is ringing up to accept or decline an invitation for some sort of celebration. Make notes while you listen on details such as:

   a) who is ringing whom,
   b) what celebration the invitation is for,
   c) the day and date of the celebration,
   d) the time at which the celebration starts,
   e) whether the person accepts or declines the invitation and the reason, if it is given.

B Now read these five invitation cards carefully. On the basis of your notes, decide which invitation card goes with which telephone conversation.

a

Einladung

Bitte
den Termin
notieren...

am *5 Dezember*

wird bei *Roland*

in der Pirnbaum Str. 27

in Wiesbaden

ab *19* Uhr gefeiert!

Bitte Antwort unter Tel.:

Wiesbaden 25478

1763-1

b

Am _Montag, den 9. Juni_

um _18_ Uhr

feiern wir

Steffis
16. Geburtstag
und laden _Dich_ herzlich ein

Familie Soest
Leibnitzallee 34

Bochum den _25. Mai_ 19___

u.A.w.g.

41-H2881

c

Am _Samstag, den 5. April_

um _14_ Uhr

feiern wir

die Verlobung von
Karl-Heinz und Jutta
und laden _Dich_ herzlich ein

Familie Räthe
Hauptstraße 221

Osnabrück den _1. März_ 19___

41-H2849

u.A.w.g.

d

Am _Mittwoch, den 31. Dezember_

um _ab 22_ Uhr

feiern wir

Silvester bei
Volker
und laden _Dich_ herzlich ein

Familie Brandt
Grobiusweg 3

Dedenburg den _1. Dezember_ 19___

u.A.w.g.

41-H2843

Bitte mit-bringen

STIMMUNG   GUTE LAUNE   WITZ   DURST

HUMOR   FROHSINN

e

ANLASS _Abiturfeier_

ORT _Ottostraße 39_

DATUM _Freitag, den 23. Juni_

ZEIT _ab 19.30 Uhr_

GASTGEBER _Sven_

HERZLICH WILLKOMMEN

Jetzt bist du dran!

A Your partner invites you to a party. He/she asks, for example:

  a) Möchtest du zu meiner Geburtstagsparty kommen?
  b) Hier ist eine Einladung zu meiner Party am Samstag. Kannst du kommen?
  c) Ich habe eine Party am Samstag. Möchtest du kommen?

You have to make sure that you find out exactly when and where the party is being given:

  a) Wann ist denn die Party?
  b) Um wieviel Uhr fängt die Party denn an?
  c) Wie spät soll ich denn kommen?
  d) Wo findet denn die Party statt?
  e) Wo ist denn die Party?

B Now decline the invitation and give a reason why you cannot come, for example:

  a) Es tut mir leid, aber ich kann nicht kommen. Am Samstag besuche ich meine Oma.
  b) Vielen Dank für die Einladung, aber ich bin am Sonntag schon zu einer Party eingeladen.
  c) Ich kann leider nicht kommen. Ich muß an dem Abend meine Brieffreundin aus England vom Flughafen abholen.

Jetzt schreibst du!

A You have decided that you are going to have a party sometime within the next ten days. Turn to worksheet A of this chapter and fill in the invitation card at the top of the sheet in a similar fashion to those you read at the beginning of the chapter. Decide what kind of party you are going to have, and when and where it is going to take place.

B You want to make your party a big success, you therefore decide to invite as many people as possible. Enter their names in your *Gästeliste*.

C You are really fond of parties and people like to invite you to them. Fill in the diary pages on the worksheet with as many invitations to parties as you can think of.

D Circulate around your class and invite your guests to your party. Whenever you invite someone, give details about what the party is for and when and where it is to be held. Your chosen guests should accept the invitation if they are free on that day and decline it, giving a reason, if he/she cannot make it. Keep a record of who has been able to accept your invitation.

Geburtstagsgrüße

It is your penfriend's birthday and you wish to send him/her a card. Look at this selection and choose the most appropriate one, bearing in mind that you will not be able to be present on the day and that you have asked a mutual friend to deliver your card.

3.

1.

ZUM GEBURTSTAG

möchte ich mit Dir
bei JEDEM GUTEN WUNSCH
das Glas erheben...

2.

Zum Geburtstag

GLÜCK

Glück und Freude braucht
der Mensch zum Leben

ROUSINA

Drum sollst Du Gutes essen
und auch einen heben

HEITERKEIT

Behalte den Humor sei froh
und heiter und mach bis
100 JAHR'
so weiter

4.

DEIN GEBURTSTAG IST
EIN HÖCHST ANSTRENGENDES
EREIGNIS FÜR MICH!

SCHULZ

5.

Eine Geburtstagsparty

Your Swiss penfriend Maria has written you a letter in which she describes a party she has been to. Read it carefully.

Vokabeln
Glace – (Swiss usage) ice cream
der Schlagrahm – (Swiss/Austrian usage) whipped cream
klitschenaß – (slang) wet through

Lieber Faisal,

Danke für Deinen lieben Brief. Ich freue mich, daß es Dir so gut geht und daß Du mit Deinen Freunden so viele interessante Dinge unternimmst. Ich war kürzlich auf einer tollen Party eingeladen, die Geburtstagsparty meiner Freundin Karin.

Karin hatte alle acht Mädchen aus unserer Klasse zu sich nach Hause eingeladen. Wir haben ihr geholfen, den Tisch fertigzumachen und zu schmücken. Zum Essen haben wir uns selbst Fondue gekocht, und zum Nachtisch gab es Glace mit viel Schlagrahm!

Die Party fand gerade zur Fasnacht statt, und da haben wir uns natürlich alle verkleidet. Draußen auf der Straße fand gerade ein Fasnachtsumzug statt. Wir haben uns dann auch auf die Straße gewagt und haben alle miteinander zu der Musik getanzt. Leider fing es plötzlich ganz feste an zu regnen. Wir sind alle klitschenaß geworden.

Abends sind wir noch zum Hotel Hecht gegangen. Dort gab es Musik und Tanz für die Maskierten. Wir tanzten, bis wir müde waren und uns die Füße weh täten. Es war eine tolle Party, sage ich Dir.

Ich muß jetzt schließen, denn es ist Abendbrotzeit. Schreib bald mal wieder.
Viele liebe Grüße
Maria

Jetzt schreibst du!

Imagine you were a guest at Karin's party. Write a short letter home to your friend, in English, telling him/her what a nice time you had, what you did, what you had to eat, etc. Include at least seven facts.

B. Weihnachten

You have asked your penfriend what Christmas is like in Germany. She shows you the page in her diary where she has written down what Christmas Eve was like for her last year. Read her diary entry and move on to "Kapiert?".

24. Dezember

Edda

Heute morgen bin ich ganz früh aufgestanden, weil ich noch in die Stadt fahren mußte, um noch einige kleine Geschenke zu kaufen. Vati und Jürgen hatten einen Weihnachtsbaum aus dem Wald geholt. Nach dem Mittagessen ist jeder auf sein Zimmer gegangen, um die Geschenke schön einzupacken und Weihnachtskarten zu schreiben. Ins Wohnzimmer durften wir nicht gehen, weil Vati dort den Weihnachtsbaum geschmückt hat. Mutti und Vati haben dann alle Geschenke unter den Baum gelegt. Dabei haben sie Weihnachtslieder vom Radio gehört. Als es dunkel war, hat Vati die Kerzen angezündet und uns heruntergerufen. Wir haben unsere Geschenke auch unter den Baum gelegt. Dann haben wir alle ein Glas Wein getrunken, uns "Frohe Weihnachten" gewünscht und einige Weihnachtslieder gesungen. Jeder hat dann geholfen, den Tisch zu decken, und wir hatten unser Weihnachtsessen. Es war wirklich toll: erst hatten wir Melone mit Sherry, dann eine Hühnersuppe mit Ei. Als Hauptgericht gab es eine Pute mit verschiedenen Gemüsen und Salzkartoffeln. Zum Nachtisch gab es dann Schokoladenpudding mit Vanillesauce. Dann endlich war es Zeit für die Bescherung. Alle waren damit beschäftigt, die Geschenke auszupacken. Wir waren alle sehr glücklich und zufrieden. Jetzt war es Zeit, in die Kirche zu gehen. Wir gehen sonst nicht sehr oft in die Kirche, aber zur Christmette gehen wir jedes Jahr. In der Kirche ist immer eine wunderschöne Krippe aufgebaut, und es macht Spaß, mit allen Leuten viele Weihnachtslieder zu singen. Erst nach Mitternacht sind wir wieder zu Hause gewesen, und ich bin völlig müde ins Bett gefallen.

Vokabeln

die Bescherung – giving of Christmas presents
das Hauptgericht – main course
die Pute – turkey
die Christmette – Midnight Service/Mass

Kapiert?

24th December: correct me if I'm wrong! Note down in your notebook
whether the following statements are correct or false.

1. Your friend was able to have a lie-in.
2. Her father and brother had bought a Christmas tree.
3. After dinner they all had a nap.
4. While the presents were being put under the tree, they listened to
   heavy-metal on the radio.
5. Because it was dark, they put the lights on.
6. They always unwrap their presents before the meal.
7. The dinner included turkey soup.
8. They went to church because they are regular attenders.
9. What a drag it is for your friend to have to go to church!
10. They get home shortly before midnight.

Weihnachtskarten

Here is a selection of German Christmas cards and greetings. Read them
carefully. Note the different ways of saying "Happy Christmas".

1.

Frohe
Weihnachten
und viel Glück
im neuen Jahr

wünscht

Familie Nüsser

2.

Frohe Weihnacht und ein gutes neues Jahr

3.

... und grüß
alle
schön!

4.

Frohe Weihnacht
und ein glückliches neues Jahr

5.

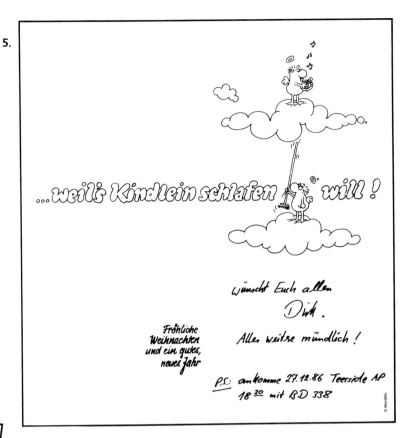

... weil's Kindlein schlafen will !

wünscht Euch allen

Dirk.

Fröhliche
Weihnachten
und ein gutes,
neues Jahr

Alles weitere mündlich !

P.S.: ankomme 27.12.86 Teesside AP
18 ³⁰ mit BD 338

6.

Dearest Marie, Dieter &
Thomas,

Zum
Weihnachtsfest
und zum
neuen Jahr
die besten
Wünsche

love Ann, Uli, Robert &
Victoria.
X

7.

Frohe Weihnachten und ein gutes neues Jahr

8.

Herzliche Weihnachtsgrüße und die besten Wünsche zum neuen Jahr

9.

Gesegnete Weihnacht
und ein gutes neues Jahr

Jetzt bist du dran!

Your German penfriend asks you a number of questions about the way you celebrate Christmas in England. Answer him/her in German.

1. Um wieviel Uhr stehst du Weihnachten auf?
2. Wann ist die Bescherung bei dir?
3. Was für Geschenke hast du letztes Jahr bekommen?
4. Was hast du deinem Vater oder deiner Mutter geschenkt?
5. Versteckt ihr die Geschenke unter dem Bett oder sonstwo?
6. Habt ihr einen echten oder einen künstlichen Weihnachtsbaum?
7. Wer schmückt den Weihnachtsbaum?
8. Gehst du zur Kirche?
9. Was machst du denn sonst vor dem Essen?
10. Um wieviel Uhr ißt du?
11. Was ißt man alles zu Weihnachten?
12. Was machst du am Nachmittag?
13. Siehst du zu Weihnachten viel fern?
14. Freust du dich auf Weihnachten?
15. Was gefällt dir an Weihnachten am besten?

Here are some expressions which you may find useful when you talk about Christmas in Britain:

turkey – der Truthahn
Brussel sprouts – der Rosenkohl
Happy New Year – Guten Rutsch ins neue Jahr!
                – Frohes Neues Jahr!
Roast potatoes – die gebratenen Kartoffeln
Christmas pudding – der Plumpudding

Jetzt schreibst du!

You have just received a letter from your penpal telling you everything he/she did on Christmas Day. You would like to reply immediately, but you are too busy at the moment. So you merely jot down some notes in German on the kind of things you want to mention. Include some of the following points in your notes:

a) what Christmas was like, i.e. whether you enjoyed it,
b) what you did on Christmas Day in the morning,
c) when you opened your presents, what you received,
d) what you had for dinner,
e) what you did in the afternoon, whether you visited someone or stayed at home, whether you played any games, etc.,
f) don't forget New Year greetings.

C. Eine Hochzeit

Hochzeitsglückwünsche

Look at these wedding congratulations and cards. Which words for *wedding* can you find?

1. Zur Hochzeit
herzliche Glückwünsche

2. Zur Vermählung herzlichen Glückwunsch

3. DEM BRAUTPAAR
HOCHZEITS-HAUS
ALLE GUTEN WÜNSCHE

Hör zu! ❷

A On German radio, you hear the following interview with a young couple about to be married. Listen to what they say and state whether, in what order and when the following events will take place:

a) honeymoon,
b) coffee and cake,
c) sending invitations,
d) evening disco,
e) *Polterabend*,
f) church wedding,
g) meal in restaurant,
h) wedding in registry office.

B Now try and explain some of these events in your own words.

DIE SCHULE

UNIT 5

πr $\sqrt{55}$

$2 + 2 = ?$

In this unit you will practise:
▷ talking about your subjects, teachers and activities,
▶ describing your school,
▷ describing your daily routine.
You will find out:
▶ a little about schools in Germany.

A. Der Schultag

Hör zu! ❶

Some German pupils will tell you which school they go to. Listen to what they say and make notes. Then copy the following grid into your notebook and fill it in.

	Type of school	Class	One other fact mentioned
1. 2. 3. etc.			

Jetzt bist du dran!

You are a German exchange student who wishes to learn something about the school system in England. Ask your partner the following questions, then change roles.

1. Was für eine Schule besuchst du?
2. Um wieviel Uhr fängt deine Schule an?
3. Wieviele Stunden habt ihr am Tag?
4. Wie lange dauert eine Stunde?
5. Wieviele Pausen hast du?
6. Wann darfst du nach Hause gehen?
7. Hast du samstags Schule?
8. Wie oft hast du Sport in der Schule?

Ich gehe zur Realschule

Your friend Wayne shows you a letter he has just received from his friend Selim in Germany. Read it carefully.

Freiburg, den 5. November.

Lieber Wayne,

Morgen ist schon wieder Montag. Am
Wochenende vergeht die Zeit immer so
schnell, findest Du nicht? Ich schreibe
nur ganz kurz, weil ich noch Hausaufgaben machen muß.

Unsere Schule fängt schon um 8:00
Uhr morgens an, und um 13:30 Uhr
ist die letzte Stunde zu Ende. Zwischen-
durch haben wir zwei große Pausen
und ein paar kurze Pausen. Meine
Schule ist eine Realschule und hat ungefähr 650 Schüler. Wir müssen samstags
auch zur Schule gehen. Das ärgert mich
unheimlich. Ich möchte dann immer
viel lieber mal ausschlafen.

Bei Dir ist das anders, nicht? Ihr
habt doch samstags immer frei, oder?
Wie viele Schüler hat denn Deine Schule?
Meine Englischlehrerin hat gesagt, daß
Ihr immer so eine komische Uniform
tragen müßt. Stimmt das?

So, jetzt muß ich aber meine Hausaufgaben machen. Bis bald, schreib
bitte bald zurück.
        Viele liebe Grüße,
                Selim.

Jetzt schreibst du!

Write a letter to your penpal telling him/her:

a) what sort of school you go to,
b) when school starts and finishes,
c) how many lessons and breaks you have,
d) whether or not you have Saturday school,
e) whether or not you like school.

B. Die Stunden

Hör zu! ❷

You will hear seven short extracts from various lessons. Listen carefully. After each one, write down in your notebook the German name of the lesson which is being taught.

Jetzt bist du dran!

Imagine you are the German penfriend of your partner. Ask him/her about the subjects he/she studies at school. Then change roles.

1. Welche Fächer lernst du in der Schule?
2. Welche Fächer hast du gern?
3. Welche Fächer magst du nicht?
4. Was ist dein Lieblingsfach?
5. Seit wann lernst du . . . ?
6. Möchtest du auch . . . lernen?
7. In welchen Fächern machst du das GCSE–Examen?

Ernst

Der Stundenplan

You will shortly be doing a school exchange and you have just received a letter from your exchange partner Ernst Pfeifer. He has sent you his school timetable so that you can make any preparations you want. Your father is very interested in what you will be doing at school in Germany and asks you some questions.

	Montag	Dienstag	Mittwoch	Donnerstag	Freitag	Samstag
8 - 8⁴⁵	Englisch	Religion	Französisch	Französisch	Chemie	Mathe
8⁵⁰ 9²⁵	Biologie	Religion	Französisch	Mathe	Chemie	Musik
9³⁵-10⁴⁰	Physik	Geschichte	Musik	Sport	Latein	Politik
10⁴⁵-11²⁰	Physik	Latein	Mathe	Sport	Biologie	Englisch
11⁴⁵-12²⁰	Latein	Englisch	Deutsch	Deutsch	Französisch	
12³⁵-13²⁰	Deutsch		Politik	Geschichte		
13³⁰-14¹⁵						
14¹⁵-15⁰⁰		Sport				
15⁰⁰-15⁴⁵		Sport				

Answer him:

1. On which days do you go to school?
2. How many lessons will you have per week?
3. How many of these will be German lessons?
4. Will you be able to attend any French classes?
5. Are there any subjects which you do not study in Britain?
6. At what time do you start in the mornings?
7. At what time do you finish?
8. There are two lessons entered on Tuesday afternoon. What are they?
9. What do you have on Wednesdays at 10.45 a.m.?
10. Will you have any computing lessons?

Jetzt schreibst du!

You wish to send your timetable to your exchange partner in Germany. You have decided to write it out for him/her in German so that his/her parents will be able to understand it. So write out your own timetable in German.

Jetzt bist du dran!

You have spent your first day in your German exchange school. The teacher was dictating the timetable to you in class. You managed to take some subjects down, but you also left many gaps. So you ask your exchange partner to help you complete your timetable.

Work in pairs. Ask your exchange partner (your partner) for the missing lessons on your timetable and complete section A of worksheet A of this unit. (Your partner gives you the answer from section B). Then change roles. This time you supply your partner with the missing information for his/her timetable (section B of the worksheet) from your timetable. Check your worksheets at the end. You should each have one complete timetable!

Ask, for example:

1. Was habe ich am Dienstag in der ersten Stunde?
2. Was habe ich am Mittwoch nach der 1. Pause?
3. Was habe ich am Freitag vor der Englischstunde?
   etc.

C. Die Fächer

Das Zeugnis

Your exchange partner Heidrun's school is the *Adam-Kraft-Gymnasium* in Schwabach. She has shown you her school report. Read it carefully on the following page.

Adam-Kraft-Gymnasium Schwabach

Mathematisch-naturwissenschaftliches, Neusprachliches und Humanistisches Gymnasium

Jahreszeugnis

Heidrun Leberle

(Sämtliche Vornamen, Familienname)

geboren am *23. Juli* 19*75* zu *Starnberg*,

Kreis *Starnberg* *katholischen* Bekenntnisses,

hat im Schuljahr 19*88*/*89* die Klasse *10* des ~~Math.-nat.~~/Neuspr./~~Humanist.~~ Gymnasiums besucht.

Leistungen:

Religionslehre	*sehr gut*	Gemeinschaftskunde	
Deutsch	*gut*	Geschichte	*gut*
Englisch	*gut*	Erdkunde	*befriedigend*
(. Fremdsprache)		Sozialkunde	*gut*
Französisch	*befriedigend*		
(. Fremdsprache)		~~Wirtschaftslehre~~	
Latein	*befriedigend*		
(. Fremdsprache)		Kunsterziehung	*sehr gut*
~~Griechisch~~		Musik	*gut*
(. Fremdsprache)		Leibeserziehung	*gut*
Mathematik	*ausreichend*		
Naturwissenschaften			
Physik	*mangelhaft*		
Chemie	*ausreichend*		
Biologie	*befriedigend*		

Die Erlaubnis zum Vorrücken in die nächsthöhere Klasse hat ~~er~~ — sie — erhalten.
~~Der Schüler~~ Die Schülerin ist damit zum Eintritt in die Oberstufe eines Gymnasiums berechtigt (Oberstufenreife).

Schwabach, den *24. 6.* 19*89*

Der Direktor:

[signature]

(S)

Der Klaßleiter:

Waldherr O.St.R.

Notenstufen: sehr gut, gut, befriedigend, ausreichend, mangelhaft, ungenügend.

Form. H 426 g

Kapiert?

Your older brother is very interested in Heidrun's report, but he does not speak any German. Answer his questions:

1. Which are Heidrun's best subjects?
2. Which are her worst subjects?
3. On what date was her report issued?
4. Does the report state Heidrun's date of birth?
5. Does it give any other personal details about her?
6. What class will Heidrun be in next year?
7. How well has Heidrun done? Order her subjects according to how well she has done, starting with her best subject.

Eine Schülerin aus der BRD erzählt

Your teacher, Gary Fowler, has written to Yvonne, the daughter of a friend of his in Germany, and asked her to tell him about the school system in Germany. He has given each of you a copy of Yvonne's reply. Read it carefully below and overleaf.

Wuppertal, den 3. September

Lieber Gary,

Heute will ich endlich Deine Fragen zu unserem Schulsystem beantworten. Wie Du weißt, gehe ich hier in Wuppertal aufs Gymnasium. Im allgemeinen hat man erst vier Jahre Grundschule, dann sechs Jahre Realschule oder neun Jahre Gymnasium – zusammen also entweder zehn oder dreizehn Jahre. Ich bin jetzt in der 10. Klasse. Die Schule fängt morgens um 8.00 Uhr an und geht bis 13.20 Uhr oder 14.00 Uhr. Wir müssen jeden Tag, also auch samstags, zur Schule. Morgens haben wir zwei große Pausen und kleine Pausen von fünf Minuten zwischen jeder Stunde, damit wir die Klassenräume wechseln können. Mittagessen gibt es bei uns in der Schule nicht. Darüber bin ich ganz schön froh, denn ich möchte nachmittags keinen Unterricht haben.

Mein Stundenplan ist ziemlich hart: ich habe insgesamt 35 Stunden in der Woche, und jede zweite Woche noch zwei Stunden extra für Sport. Aber das ist auf jeden Fall nicht langweilig. Wir haben jeden Tag verschiedene Fächer und in jedem Fach einen anderen Lehrer – das gibt eine Menge Abwechslung.

Ich habe in der fünften Klasse Englisch als erste Fremdsprache angefangen. In der siebten Klasse kam dann noch Französisch dazu. Ab der neunten Klasse können wir einige Fächer als Wahlfach belegen. Ich habe Geschichte genommen. Andere haben Sport oder Geographie gewählt.

Eigentlich bin ich mit der Schule ganz zufrieden. Allerdings haben wir eine ganze Menge von langweiligen Lehrern bei uns. Ich kenne nur wenige, die uns gut unterrichten. In manchen Stunden, wie z.B. in Politik und Geschichte, paßt kein Mensch auf. Das liegt allerdings nicht am Fach, sondern einzig und allein daran, daß die Lehrer langweilig unterrichten.

Meine Lieblingsfächer sind: Sport, Englisch, Geschichte und Musik.

So, ich hoffe, daß ich Dir und Deinen Schülern mit diesem Brief geholfen habe und daß Ihr Euch jetzt eine besseres Bild vom deutschen Schulsystem machen könnt.

Tschüß und liebe Grüße
Deine

Yvonne

Vokabeln

die Abwechslung – change, variety
das Wahlfach – optional subject
belegen – (here) to take
das Fach – subject

Jetzt schreibst du!

Turn to worksheet B of this unit. Imagine you were Yvonne and fill in the questionnaire the way you think she would have answered.

IN DEN FERIEN

UNIT **6**

In this unit you will practise:
▷ discussing holiday preferences,
▶ contacting others by letter and telephone,
▷ asking for directions and information,
▶ interpreting weather forecasts.

A. Unterwegs

Hör zu! ❶

A number of German people will talk about where they go for their holidays. Listen carefully and make notes. Copy the grid below into your notebook and complete it.

	Destination	Length of stay	Reason for going there
1. 2. 3. etc.			

Jetzt bist du dran!

A Your exchange group leader has asked you to find out where young people in Germany like to go on holiday. Ask three of your German friends (your classmates will assume this role) how they hope to spend their holiday this year and what they did last year. You have to find out from each one of them:

This summer	Last summer
a) where they hope to go, b) how long they hope to stay, c) whether they are going alone, d) their reason for going there.	e) where they went, f) how long they stayed, g) with whom they went, h) their reason for having gone there.

B When you have concluded your interviews, you report back to your exchange group leader (your teacher). Here are some suggestions for your report:

Karl möchte nach . . . fahren.
Karl hat vor, nach . . . zu fahren.
Karl hat beschlossen, nach . . . zu fahren.

Er fährt mit . . .
Er fährt allein.
Er fährt dahin, weil/das Wetter schön ist.
             /er gern Wassersport treibt.
             /es so billig ist.
             /seine Tante dort wohnt.

Er möchte zwei Nächte da verbringen/bleiben.
Er hat vor, eine Nacht da zu verbringen.
Er hat beschlossen, eine Woche da zu verbringen.

The second half of your report could go something like this:

Susan ist letztes Jahr/im vergangenen Jahr nach . . . gefahren.
Sie hat zwei Wochen da verbracht.
Sie ist mit . . . gefahren.
Sie ist dahin gefahren, weil . . .

Hör zu! ❷

Your school is being visited by a German exchange group. They have asked a number of you about your plans for your next holidays and the travel arrangements you have made. Elizabeth, Craig, Justin, Sarah, and Jonathan describe their plans. Listen to what they say. Copy the following grid into your notebook and tick the appropriate columns.

	alone	not alone	plane	ferry	car	train	other
Elizabeth Craig Justin Sarah Jonathan							

Reisepläne

Read these four postcards, in which people inform their friends about their travel arrangements. Then answer the questions underneath.

1. Lieber Karl,
Am Dienstag den 21.6. Komme ich um 22.10 in Köln Hauptbahnhof an. Wenn ich Schwierigkeiten habe, rufe ich Dich an. Hast Du noch mein Foto? Ich bin etwas größer geworden, aber sonst habe ich mich nicht verändert.
Ich freue mich sehr auf meinen Besuch.
Bis bald
Wayne.

2.

Liebe Bärbel,

Es tut mir Leid, aber ich mußte meine Pläne etwas ändern. Ich schaffe es nicht, mit dem ersten Zug von London zu fahren. An dem Tag muß mein Vater leider arbeiten. Er fährt mich aber nach Feierabend direkt zum Bahnhof. Ich fahre dann um 20.05 Uhr von London Victoria Station und bin um 08.25 Uhr am nächsten Morgen, d.h. Donnerstag, in Koblenz. Kannst Du mich noch abholen? Wenn nicht, ruf mich bitte an. Viele freundliche Grüße,

Anne

3.

Liebe Marita,

Es sind jetzt nur noch vier Wochen, bis wir uns sehen. Ich habe gestern mein Flugticket gekauft. Ich fliege am Donnerstag, den 28. Juli von Manchester direkt nach Zürich. Das Flugzeug kommt um 16.40 Uhr an. Wie fahre ich dann vom Flughafen weiter? Holt mich Dein Vater oder Deine Mutter ab, oder fahre ich besser mit dem Taxi?
Ich freue mich sehr darauf, Dich wiederzusehen.
    Deine Penny

4.

Lieber Gareth,

Nur noch zwei Wochen und ich bin bei Dir in Newcastle. Weißt du was? Ich kann mit dem Schiff direkt nach Newcastle fahren. Ich fahre zuerst mit dem Zug von Hamburg nach Esjberg in Dänemark und dann mit dem Schiff. Die Überfahrt dauert fast einen ganzen Tag! Die Fähre kommt um 15.30 Uhr am Mittwoch, den 13. August an. Hoffentlich kannst Du mich abholen. Wenn nicht, was mache ich dann am besten? Du wirst mich sicher erkennen, obwohl mein Haar jetzt kürzer ist. Ich werde meinen blauen Anorak tragen.
    Schöne Grüße an Deine Schwester und Deine Eltern.
        Dein Hugo

Kapiert?

1. What travel arrangements has each person made?
2. What questions do they ask?
3. How can Wayne and Hugo be recognised?

Hör zu! ❸

Listen to the following telephone conversations and write down what travel arrangements have been made.

Jetzt bist du dran!

You have made arrangements to travel to Germany. You ˙ ing your friend in Germany (your partner takes this part) and tell him/heı the details of your journey and your arrival. Carry out the following roleplays, acting out each of the situations given at least once.

Mode of travel:	Train	Coach	Air	Ferry
Date:	30 May	Tuesday	8 Dec	14 July
Place of arrival:	Main station	Outside city hall	Airport	Hamburg
Time of arrival:	13.30	21.15	07.10	18.23
Recognition:	Red anorak	Yellow scarf	Has glasses now	British flag on rucksack

Jetzt schreibst du!

Write a postcard to your penfriend, giving him/her the details of your travel arrangements to Germany. Include the following points:

a) how you travel,
b) the day and date of your departure,
c) the day and date of your arrival,
d) the place you will arrive at,
e) how you may be recognised.

Schildersprache

You are likely to see some or all of the following signs when you travel on holiday abroad. What does each mean?

1.

2.

3.

4.

B. Wie komme ich am besten . . . ?

Touristeninformation

Look at these photographs and read the signs.

a) Do you know what they stand for?

b) Who can go there?

c) Why do they go there?

d) What sort of things can they pick up there?

Hör zu! ❹

Listen to the following conversation which takes place in the tourist information office in Cologne. Answer the questions in section a) and fill in the gaps in sections b) and c). Copy these sentences into your notebook.

a) How long has the tourist been in Cologne?
   What does he want?
   How much does it cost?

b) The tourist is interested in . . .
   There are lots of/several/two . . . in Cologne.

c) Complete the following instructions:
   We are here in front of the cathedral. When you go out, turn . . . You go through the . . . Then take the . . . street on the . . . It's called *Minoritenstraße*. The museum is on the . . . It is . . . to find.

Hör zu! ❺

You will hear a number of people asking for and receiving directions. Listen carefully. Note down where each speaker wants to go and how he/she can get there.

Jetzt bist du dran!

A Work in pairs. Turn to worksheet A of this unit. On it, you see eight small maps. The "x" indicates your present position. Ask your partner how you get to the place shown on each map. Make sure that his/her instructions will really get you there – then change roles.

B Look at the map of *Würzburg* below. On it you will see ten places
marked by numbers 1–10. However, the map does not provide a key.
Agree on a list of ten possible places with your partner, e.g.: *Hotel,
Post, Kino, Bank, Theater, Schloß, Kunstgallerie, Café, Jugendherberge,
Universität.* Then write out your keys to the map separately, giving the
places agreed on the numbers 1–10, without your partner being able to
see. Now your partner has to find out in which order you listed the
places by asking you how to get to each individual place from the
starting position indicated on the map. Change roles. When you have
finished, check to see whether you have got it right.

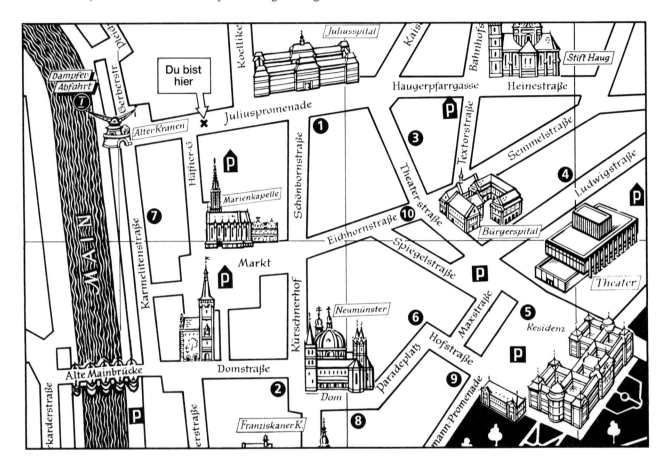

Possible questions:

> Wie komme ich am besten zum/zur . . . ?
> Wo ist bitte . . . ?
> Wissen Sie, wo . . . ist?

Possible answers:

> Gehen Sie rechts/links/geradeaus.
> Nehmen Sie die erste/zweite/dritte Straße rechts/links.
> . . . ist an der rechten/linken Seite,
>   gleich neben der Post/gegenüber dem Theater/zwischen dem Gasthaus
>   und der Bäckerei.
> Gehen Sie an der . . ./ am . . . vorbei.

C. Das Wetter

Wie ist das Wetter?

Look at the pictures below, then read the list of captions. Match each caption with the correct picture.

a) es blitzt   d) die Sonne scheint   g) es schneit
b) es donnert   e) es regnet   h) es hagelt
c) es ist windig   f) es ist neblig   i) es friert

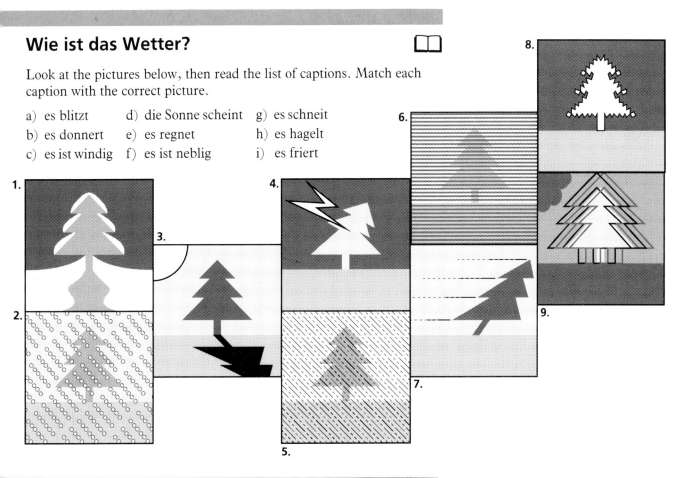

Hör zu! ❻

You are on holiday with your parents in Germany and listen to the international weather forecast. Listen carefully and fill in the gaps in this text so that you can tell your parents what the weather is expected to be like in the most popular holiday places.

1. In Southern Germany there will be . . . at the beginning of the day. The mountains will frequently be . . . Maximum temperatures . . .

2. Austria and . . . In the east it will be very . . . and from time to time there will be . . . or . . . As the weekend approaches, the weather will . . . with isolated thunderstorms in the . . . or . . . Temperatures in the Alps . . .

3. Italy, . . ., Balearics and . . . In the north . . . In the south . . .

4. Czechoslovakia and . . . Mostly bright to . . . and predominantly . . . Temperatures . . .

5. Yugoslavia. Any signs of rain?

6. Romania and . . ., . . . and . . . Temperatures . . .

7. . . . and Turkey. On the . . ., temperatures up to . . .

8. . . . and . . . On the coast . . . Inland . . .

9. Spain. In the north . . . Water temperatures . . .

Das Wetter heute und morgen

You read the following weather forecast in a German newspaper.

das wetter heute und morgen

Wetterlage

Ausläufer eines skandinavischen Sturmtiefs streifen Schleswig-Holstein. Dabei wird zunächst milde, später merklich kältere Meeresluft herangeführt.

Vorhersage für heute

Stark bewölkt bis bedeckt und zeitweise Regen. Gebietsweise noch diesig. Nur örtlich kurze Bewölkungsauflockerungen. Tageshöchsttemperaturen 3 bis 6 Grad. Tiefste Nachtwerte zum Freitag hin nur wenig darunter. Mäßige bis frische Winde aus Südwest bis West.

Aussichten für morgen

Übergang zu wechselnder Bewölkung. Vereinzelt Regenschauer. Bei auflebenden und Nordwest drehenden Winden wieder Temperaturrückgang.

Temperaturen u. Niederschläge

Temperaturangaben für gestern 13.00 Uhr MEZ, Niederschlagsmenge für 24 Stunden

Kiel	+	1	Grad	
Schleswig	+	1	Grad	
Insel Fehmarn	+	2	Grad	
List auf Sylt	+	3	Grad	
Hamburg		0	Grad	
Berlin	+	6	Grad	
Bonn	+	6	Grad	
Frankfurt	+	4	Grad	
München	+	2	Grad	
Paris	+	4	Grad	14 mm
Rom	+	17	Grad	
Stockholm	+	2	Grad	
Oslo	+	4	Grad	
Helsinki	−	3	Grad	0,6 mm
London	+	4	Grad	0,2 mm

DEUTSCHER WETTERDIENST
Vorhersagekarte für den 1. März 84, 7 Uhr

○ wolkenlos	◐ Windstille
◑ heiter	Nordwind 10 km/h
◔ halb bedeckt	Ostwind 20 km/h
◕ wolkig	Südwind 30 km/h
● bedeckt	Westwind 40 km/h
≡ Nebel	9 Niseln
● Regen	▼ Schauer
⬡ Gewitter	Niederschlagsgebiet

Warmfront
Okklusion
Luftströmung
Kaltfront am Boden
in der Höhe
warm
kalt
H Hochdruckzentrum
T Tiefdruckzentrum
Hektopascal

Temperatur in Grad Celsius

Sonne und Mond

am 2. März 1984

Sonnenaufgang	07.06 Uhr
Sonnenuntergang	17.59 Uhr
Mondaufgang	07.39 Uhr
Monduntergang	17.27 Uhr

Ebbe und Flut

2. März	Hochw.		Niedrigw.	
Husum	01.54	14.17	08.41	20.46
Büsum	00.36	13.02	06.58	19.19
Brunsbüttel	02.03	14.30	09.17	21.28

Angaben der Wetterstation Kiel, Berechnung des Hydrogr. Instituts Hamburg (Zahlenangaben ohne Gewähr)

Kapiert?

Your mum and dad are keen to know what the weather is to be like for their last few days in Germany. Can you help them?

1. Is it going to get warmer?
2. Would it be a good idea to sunbathe today? Give reasons.
3. Will it be windy?
4. What about tomorrow? Cloudy? Rainy? Windy? Temperatures?
5. What was the hottest place yesterday?
6. What was the coldest?
7. At what time will you have to turn your lights on?
8. What time is high tide in Büsum in the evening?
9. What time is low tide in Brunsbüttel in the morning?

D. Die Ankunft

Hör zu! ❼

You will hear five people commenting on their journey. Listen and make notes:

a) How did these people travel?
b) What made their journey pleasant or unpleasant?

Jetzt bist du dran!

You have just arrived at your penfriend's. Your hosts ask you what the journey was like. Carry out the roleplays with your partner.

1. Say that your journey was very pleasant. Mention two things that you did during the journey. Say that you always enjoy travelling with this form of transport.
2. Say that the journey was awful. Mention two reasons why it was awful. Say that you'll never use this method of transport again.

Wie war die Reise?	Was hast du während der Reise gemacht?
ganz gut ein bißchen langweilig ziemlich anstrengend furchtbar sehr stürmisch nicht sehr gut ich war seekrank	gelesen geschlafen geplaudert aus dem Fenster geschaut Kreuzworträtsel gelöst

FERIENUNTERKUNFT

In this unit you will practise:

▷ booking accommodation in a hotel, a youth hostel and a campsite,

▶ settling your bill.

A. Im Hotel

Hör zu! ❶

During your stay in Germany, some friends of your exchange partner tell you where they stayed during their last holiday. Listen to what they say. Whenever your teacher stops the tape, write down the following information about each one of them:

a) the form of accommodation used,

b) the speaker's opinion of it.

Jetzt bist du dran!

You knew your German would come in useful. The following non-German-speaking people approach you in the tourist information office and ask you to recommend a hotel to them. From the advertisements, choose a suitable hotel for each person:

a) Someone travelling who would like a hotel not too far from the station at München.

b) Two friends on a shopping weekend in Munich who want to be as close to the shopping centre and the railway station as possible.

c) Business woman wanting a central hotel in a quiet situation. Room must have its own telephone.

3.

Hotel Mayerh

DACHAUER STRASSE 421, TELEFON 1 41 30
TELEX 5 24 675
Das Münchner Hotel nahe am Olympiapa

4.

Hotel Drei Löwen Münche

Erste Klasse Hotel im Herzen von München
130 Zimmer mit Bad/WC, Radio, Farbfernseher u. Minib
Restaurant, Konferenzräume, Garage, Parkplätze, Boutic
Nur 3 Gehmin. v. Hauptbhf., Flughafenbus u. Fußgängerz

8000 München 2   Telefon (0 89) 59 55 21
Schillerstr. 8   Telex 5 23 867

1.

IHRE NEUE MÜNCHNER HOTELADRESSE

1983 erbautes Haus mit 50 Betten. Sehr ruhig gelegen im Herzen von München. 5 Min. zum Rathaus – 10 Min. zum Messegelände.
Alle Zimmer mit Bad/Dusche/WC, Farbfernseher, Radio, Selbstwähltelefon, teilweise Balkon, Garten-Terrasse, Bar, Tiefgarage, Frühstücksbuffet. Genau vis-à-vis dem Europ. Patentamt.
Kohlstraße 9, Tel. 0 89/22 66 41–44, Telex 5 29 111

HOTEL Admiral MÜNCHEN

5.

HOTEL MOORBAD WETTERSTE

Grünwalder Straße 16 – 8000 München 90 – Telefon (0 89) 65 00
● über 100 Betten
● Frühstück inklusive
● Schwimmbad – Sauna
● Natur-Moor-Brei-Bad
● Damen- und Herrenfriseu
● Kosmetik-Salon
● Fitness Center/Solarium
● Tiefgarage kostenlos

2.

Hotel Uhland GARNI

Uhlandstraße 1
8000 München 2
Tel. 0 89/53 92 77
Telex 5 28 368

Das kleine Hotel an der großen Wiese

Ruhige Lage am Bavariaring, Frühstücksbuffet, Lift, Parkplätze im Hof, 10 Gehminuten zum Hbf. u. Messe, a. Zi. m. WC, DU o. Bad. ■ E 14.
Verlangen Sie bitte unseren Hauptprospekt.

30 Jahre Familien-betrieb

Hör zu! ❷

You are waiting for a friend in the lounge of a large hotel, not far from the reception desk. You overhear the following conversations which take place at the reception desk. Whenever your teacher stops the tape, write down what the person inquiring about a room requires.

So schreibt man eine Zimmerbestellung

You are the manager of a hotel and have just received this letter. Read it carefully, then summarize the contents of the letter, noting down:

a) date of arrival and departure,
b) rooms required,
c) meals required,
d) any other information you want to keep a note of.

Sehr geehrte Damen und Herren!

Im August fahre ich mit meinen Eltern nach Koblenz. Wir kommen am 13. 8. an und fahren am 19. 8. wieder ab. Haben sie während dieser Zeit noch ein Doppelzimmer und ein Einzelzimmer mit Bad/WC und womöglich Fernseher frei? Was wäre der Gesamtpreis für Halbpension?

Ich wäre auch sehr dankbar, wenn Sie uns mitteilen könnten, wie weit Sie vom Bahnhof entfernt sind und wie die Verbindungen zur Stadtmitte sind.

Ich danke Ihnen im voraus.

Mit freundlichen Grüßen.

Harald Koch

Die Antwort

In reply to an inquiry, your teacher has received this letter from the *Hotel am Ufer* in Trier. As part of your preparation for the school trip to Trier, he hands you the letter and asks you to inform the rest of the group about:

a) facilities,

b) cost,

c) any events taking place during their stay.

Trier, den 01. Februar

Betrifft: Zimmerreservierung.

Sehr geehrter Herr Chambers !

Wir danken für Ihre freundliche Anfrage und teilen Ihnen mit, daß die von Ihnen vorgesehene Reservierung zur Zeit noch möglich ist, Trier, das die älteste Stadt Deutschlands ist, feiert nämlich in diesem Jahr das Fest " TRIER 2000 Jahre alt."

Zurückkommend auf Ihre Anfrage teilen wir mit, daß alle Zimmer unseres Hauses mit Bad/Dusche + WC ausgestattet sind.

Unter Berücksichtigung der Tatsache, daß es sich um jugendliche Gäste handelt und Sie auch 2 Tage bleiben wollen biete ich Ihnen 2 Doppelzimmer und 1 Dreibettzimmer - jeweils mit Bad/Dusche + WC - einschließlich Frühstück zum Pauschalpreis von 210.00 DM je Tag = (7 x 30.- DM.) In dem Übernachtungspreis von 30.- DM je Person ist, wie bereits gesagt, das Frühstück im Wert von cirka 10.00 DM enthalten.

Der gesamte Preis für 2 Tage beträgt daher 420.00 DM.

Falls Sie an unserem Angebot interessiert sind, bitten wir um Ihre Bestellung in den nächsten 4 Wochen.

Mit freundlichen Grüßen

Anlage:
TRIER, Auskunft in Stichworten, Hotellage ist eingezeichnet.

Hotel „Am Ufer"
5500 Trier, Zurmaienerstr. 81-83

Welches Wort?

Which German word from the list a–k would you use if you wanted to book the following in a hotel?

1.	three-bedded room	a)	Bad
2.	full board	b)	Doppelzimmer
3.	single room	c)	Dreibettzimmer
4.	breakfast	d)	Dusche
5.	bath	e)	Einzelzimmer
6.	shower	f)	Frühstück
7.	half board	g)	Zweibettzimmer
8.	toilet	h)	Kinderbett
9.	cot	i)	Vollpension
10.	double room	j)	WC
11.	twin-bedded room	k)	Halbpension

Jetzt bist du dran!

Using the examples below, carry out the following roleplays with your partner. One of you assumes the role of the hotel manager, the other that of a customer ringing up to make a reservation. Change roles after each situation.

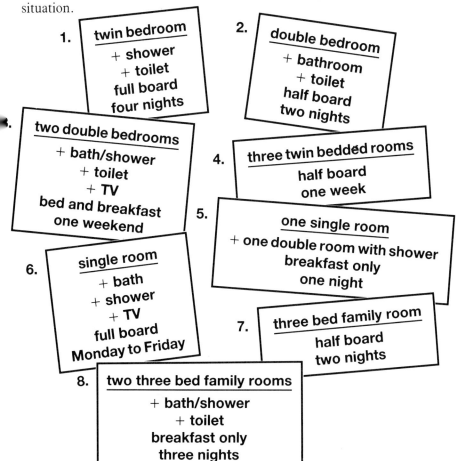

1.
twin bedroom
+ shower
+ toilet
full board
four nights

2.
double bedroom
+ bathroom
+ toilet
half board
two nights

3.
two double bedrooms
+ bath/shower
+ toilet
+ TV
bed and breakfast
one weekend

4.
three twin bedded rooms
half board
one week

5.
one single room
+ one double room with shower
breakfast only
one night

6.
single room
+ bath
+ shower
+ TV
full board
Monday to Friday

7.
three bed family room
half board
two nights

8.
two three bed family rooms
+ bath/shower
+ toilet
breakfast only
three nights

Jetzt schreibst du!

Using worksheet A of this unit, fill in the four hotel room reservation cards.
You may either use details from the cue cards on page 59 or invent your own
requirements.

Jetzt bist du dran!

Carry out these two roleplays with your partner. Once each situation has
been played through, change roles.

A You have just arrived at your hotel. You go to the reception desk and
inquire about the room you booked.

Reception: Guten Abend. Darf ich Ihnen helfen?
You: Tell him you booked a room for two nights.
Reception: Wie ist Ihr Name bitte?
You: Tell him your name and where you are from.
Reception: Ja, das stimmt. Können Sie bitte hier unterschreiben?
           Danke. Hier ist Ihr Schlüssel, Zimmer 411.
You: Ask him how to get to the room.
Reception: Ihr Zimmer befindet sich auf der vierten Etage.
You: Ask him if there is a lift.
Reception: Ja. Der Aufzug ist dort links.

B You have been to look at your room but find a number of things amiss.
You return to reception.

Reception: Guten Abend.
You: Tell the receptionist that you have just been to your room and
           the bed has not been made.
Reception: Das tut mir furchtbar leid. Das Zimmermädchen regelt das
           sofort.
You: Nor do you have any soap and the TV is broken.
Reception: Das ist ja unerhört. Ich gebe Ihnen am besten ein anderes
           Zimmer.
You: Say that would be a good idea.
Reception: Sie können Zimmer 309 haben.
You: Thank her and ask what time dinner is served.
Reception: Zwischen 7.00 und 8.30 Uhr im Restaurant.
You: What time can you have breakfast?
Reception: Zwischen 7.00 und 9.30 Uhr.
You: Say you are staying out very late and ask what time the door
           is locked.
Reception: Sie brauchen sich keine Sorgen zu machen. Hier ist immer
           jemand. Die Tür wird nicht abgeschlossen.
You: Thank her.
Reception: Es tut mir furchtbar leid, daß wir Ihnen so viele Unannehm-
           lichkeiten bereitet haben.

Die Rechnung 📖

Read the bills below and find out the following details in each case:

a) length of stay,
b) rooms occupied,
c) meals taken.

2.

1.

HOTEL »AM UFER« · TRIER
Inh.: Klemens Blasius

Herrn/Frau

Zurmaiener Straße 81-83
D-5500 TRIER
Tel. (0651) 45404/76487

_____

Chambers

_____

RECHNUNG Nr. 36   Trier, den 15. 4. 198

Zimmer Nr. 5, 7 und 16 (7 Personen)	
Ankunft: 13. 4. 1989	
Abreise: 15. 4. 1989	
2 Tag(e) Übernachtung + Frühstück a 210.-	420.00 DM
Speisen und Getränke	
Telefon	
Garage	
(Pauschalpreis für 7 Pers. = 210.-)	
Rechungs-Endbetrag enthält ..14.. % MwSt. =51.58 DM	
Betrag =	420.00 DM

Betrag dankend erhalten:
Trier, den 15. 4. 198

Hotel „Am Ufer"
5500 Trier, Zurmaienerstr. 81
    Stempel / Unterschrift

Bankkonto: Stadtsparkasse Trier Nr. 909507 (BLZ 585 500 80)

☀ **GASTHAUS SONNE**

Ramseyer   Luzernerstrasse 1   8903 Birmensdorf   Tel. 01/737 17 67

Herr
Frau
Frl.   Zi. 5, 13, 14   Datum 23. 7. 59

1	Doppelzimmer		65	-
2	Einerzimmer	9 40,-	80	-
	Frühstück			
	Mittagessen		58	20
	Dîner			
	Dessert			
	Aperitif			
	Jus			
	Wein			
	Bier			
	Mineralwasser			
	Spirituosen			
	Café			
	Extras			
	Tabac			
	Service %			
	Total		203	20

Wir danken für Ihren Besuch. Auf Wiedersehen

Hör zu! ❸ 📼

You will hear four short conversations in which a person asks for his/her hotel bill. Listen to what is being said. Whenever your teacher stops the tape, note down the phrase the customer used for asking for the bill and the method of payment chosen.

Jetzt bist du dran!

Carry out the following roleplay with your partner:

You are just about to leave your hotel and have come to reception to ask for your bill.

You: Ask for the bill, as you will be leaving soon.
Reception: Gerne, mein Herr, welches Zimmer hatten Sie?
You: Say you had room 309.
Reception: Herr/Fräulein X, ja, bitte schön; das waren zwei Übernachtungen mit Frühstück, also DM 160, und Getränke von der Minibar, DM 32, macht zusammen DM 292.
You: Surely he's made a mistake, it's only DM 192.
Reception: Oh, entschuldigen Sie bitte, natürlich. Wie möchten Sie zahlen, bitte?
You: Ask him/her if he accepts Eurocheques.
Reception: Natürlich nehmen wir Euroschecks.
You: Say thank you and goodbye.

B. Auf dem Campingplatz

Eine Platzreservierung

Your exchange partner in Germany and you wish to go cycling and camping in Austria. She has written to a campsite and booked a place for you in advance. Read her letter opposite.

Kapiert?

You tell your parents about your plans on the phone. Your mother wants to know the following details:

1. Where is the campsite?
2. How many tents are you taking?
3. How long are you going to stay at the campsite of Mrs Weiß?
4. When are you planning to arrive?
5. How are you going to get there?
6. Has Eva asked the proprietor of the campsite for any specific information?

Jetzt schreibst du!

Write a letter to a campsite containing the following points:

a) you are travelling with your parents by car,
b) you want to stay for three nights in your caravan,
c) say when you are arriving and when you are leaving,
d) ask for a pricelist, a map of the town and a list of the local attractions.

Bremen, den 28. April

Ingeborg Weiß
Hinterbergstr. 47
Obersteiermark
A-8700 Leoben

Sehr geehrte Frau Weiß!
Vom 21. Juli bis zum 28. Juli mache ich mit einer Freundin eine Radtour in Österreich. Wir haben vor, einige Tage in der Obersteiermark zu verbringen.
Könnten wir einen Platz für ein Zweipersonenzelt buchen? Wir kommen am 23. Juli an und wollen bis zum 25. Juli bleiben. Sollen wir Ihnen eine Anzahlung schicken?
Für eine Preisliste und weitere Informationen über Ihren Campingplatz und die Sehenswürdigkeiten und Veranstaltungen in der näheren Umgebung wäre ich sehr dankbar.
Mit freundlichen Grüßen,
Eva Baura

Hör zu! ❹

You will hear some conversations which take place at the booking office of a campsite. Listen carefully. Copy the information grid below into your notebook and complete it while you listen, ticking as appropriate.

	1	2	3	4
Reserviert Nicht reserviert Erwachsene Kinder Zelt Wohnwagen Auto Wie lange?				

Jetzt bist du dran!

You arrive at a campsite. Go to the registration office. The person there will help you.

Reception: Guten Tag! Kann ich Ihnen helfen?
You: Say hello. Tell the person your name and explain that you have booked a place for your tent.
Reception: Und wie ist Ihre Adresse?
You: Tell him/her.
Reception: Und wie lange wollten Sie bleiben?
You: Three nights.
Reception: Haben Sie ein Auto?
You: Tell him you have not, but you have two bicycles.
Reception: Und für wieviele Personen wäre das?
You: Two.
Reception: Gut. Bitte unterschreiben Sie dieses Anmeldeformular.

Hör zu! ❺

It is time to pay. You have joined a queue at the office of a campsite in order to pay. Listen to what the people in front of you say. Copy the grid below into your notebook and complete it with the details required.

	1	2
Site number		
No. of people		
Length of stay		
Tent or caravan		
Total cost		

Abrechnungen

Read these two campsite invoices carefully. Can you interpret them well enough to answer the questions on the next page?

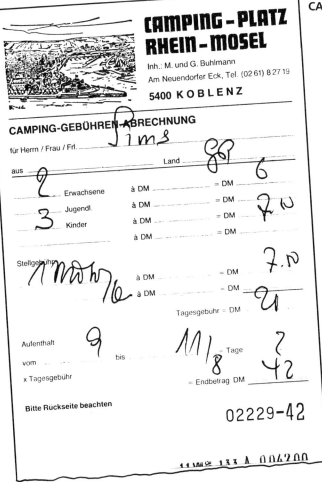

CAMPING-PLATZ RHEIN-MOSEL

Inh.: M. und G. Buhlmann
Am Neuendorfer Eck, Tel. (02 61) 8 27 19

5400 KOBLENZ

CAMPING-GEBÜHREN-ABRECHNUNG

für Herrn / Frau / Frl. _Sims_

aus _____ Land _GB_ _6_

_2_ Erwachsene à DM ____ = DM ____
_3_ Jugendl. à DM ____ = DM _7.0_
____ Kinder à DM ____ = DM ____
____ à DM ____ = DM ____

Stellgebühr

1 mor 76 à DM ____ = DM _7.0_
à DM ____ = DM ____
Tagesgebühr = DM _4_

Aufenthalt _9_ bis _11_ Tage _2_
vom ____ bis ____ _8_ _42_
x Tagesgebühr = Endbetrag DM ____

Bitte Rückseite beachten

02229-42

11 VIII 85 133 A 004200

CAMPINGPLATZ A

Campingplatz A:

1. Wieviele Personen haben gezeltet?
2. Wie lange sind sie geblieben?
3. Was kostet es pro Tag?

Campingplatz B:

1. Wann ist Herr Sims angekommen?
2. Wie lange ist er geblieben?
3. Was kostet es pro Nacht?

CAMPINGPLATZ B

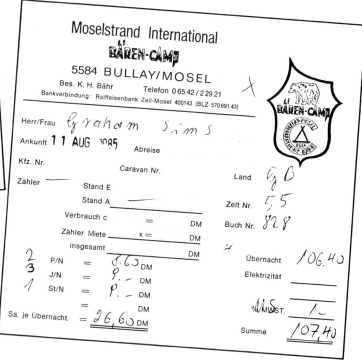

Moselstrand International
BÄREN-CAMP

5584 BULLAY/MOSEL

Bes. K. H. Bähr   Telefon 0 65 42 / 2 29 21
Bankverbindung: Raiffeisenbank Zell-Mosel 400143 (BLZ 570 691 43)

Herr/Frau _Graham Sims_
Ankunft _11 AUG 1985_   Abreise _____

Kfz. Nr. _____   Caravan Nr. _____   Land _GB_

Zähler _____   Stand E _____   Zelt Nr. _55_
   Stand A _____   Buch Nr. _828_
   Verbrauch c _____ = ____ DM
   Zähler Miete ____ x = ____ DM   Übernacht. _106.40_
   insgesamt _____ DM   Elektrizität _____

_2_ P/N = _6.60_ DM
_3_ J/N = _9.—_ DM
_1_ St/N = _8.—_ DM
   = ____ DM   % MWST. _1.—_
Sa. je Übernacht. = _26,60_ DM   Summe _107,40_

Jetzt schreibst du!

You have just received a letter from your penpal asking you what you did during the Easter holiday. Write back, telling him all about your weekend camping. Say:

a) where you went,
b) who you went with,
c) how you got there,
d) how long it took you,
e) what the weather was like,
f) whether you had difficulties getting a site, and whether you had booked,
g) what the site was like, which facilities it offered,
h) what you did and saw while you were there,
i) how much staying there cost,
j) whether you enjoyed your stay,
k) whether you would like to go there again.

C. In der Jugendherberge

Wir schreiben an die Jugendherberge

Which of these youth hostels would you choose? Write to one of them, making a booking. Here is a model letter to help you.

Lieber Herbergsvater!

Mein Freund und ich möchten zwei Nächte in Ihrer Jugendherberge verbringen. Wir kommen am 24.6. an und fahren am 26.6. wieder ab. Abendessen und Frühstück möchten wir für beide Tage. Bettwäsche brauchen wir nicht.

Wir legen einen Internationalen Postantwortschein bei.

Mit freundlichen Grüßen

Noel Lewis

Wayne Daniels.

Jugendherbergen
Youth Hostels
Auberges de jeunesse

 1

Jugendgästehaus Wien 20
Brigittenau

A-1200 Wien, Friedrich-Engels-Platz 24
Reservierung / Reservation:
A-1010 Wien, Gonzagagasse 22, Telefon 63 53 53
Voraussichtlicher Betriebsbeginn: Freitag, 13. April 1984.
Vorausbuchungen (Buchungsformular anfordern) für Termine ab dem 1. Mai 1984 ab sofort schriftlich möglich.
264 Betten, ganzjährig geöffnet; Mehrzwecksaal, geeignet für Seminare.
Nächtigung mit Frühstück 120 öS; Halbpension 160 öS; Vollpension 200 öS.

 3

Jugendgästehaus der Stadt
Wien – Hütteldorf-Hacking

A-1130 Wien, Schloßberggasse 8, Telefon 82 15 01
300 Betten, ganzjährig geöffnet.
Nächtigung mit Frühstück 87 öS.
Halb- und Vollpension möglich.

Your letter should cover the following points:

a) Are you alone or with a friend or friends?
b) Say how many nights you would like to stay.
c) Give exact dates.
d) What meals would you like?
e) Do you require bed linen?
f) Don't forget to enclose the international reply coupon!

Hör zu! ❻

Listen to the following people arriving at a youth hostel. Copy the grid below into your notebook. Can you complete it with the information a youth hostel warden would write down?

	1	2	etc.
No. in party			
Nature of party			
Meals required			
Bed linen			
Other requirements			

Jetzt bist du dran!

You have just arrived at the youth hostel. You had better sort things out with the warden. Enact the following roleplay.

Herbergsvater:	Guten Abend!
You:	Greet him and ask if he has two beds free.
Herbergsvater:	Ja. Für Jungen oder Mädchen?
You:	It's for you and your friend.
Herbergsvater:	Und wie lange möchten Sie bleiben?
You:	Only one night.
Herbergsvater:	Und möchten Sie Abendessen und Frühstück?
You:	You don't want dinner, but you would like breakfast.
Herbergsvater:	Brauchen Sie Bettwäsche?
You:	No, you've got your own.
Herbergsvater:	Darf ich die bitte mal sehen? Gut. Ihre Ausweise brauche ich noch.
You:	Hand them over.
Herbergsvater:	Gut. Gehen Sie bitte die Treppe hoch, Zimmer 4.
You:	Thank him.

Übernachtung in der Jugendherberge 📖

You wish to spend two nights in this youth hostel and are quite prepared to share a room with your friend. You would like to have a simple breakfast each morning, as well as lunch and tea on the day after your arrival, and a packed lunch on the day you leave. How much will you have to pay?

Jugendgästehaus und Lehrgangsstätte Oberwesel

Gebühren und Preise

1. Verpflegungspreise

a) Tagesverpflegung für Dauergäste bei 3 Mahlzeiten täglich. Dieser ermäßigte Preis gilt für einen Aufenthalt von mehr als 2 Tagen vom ersten Tage an.   DM 17,10

b) Verpflegungspreise für Kurzaufenthalte und zugleich Einzelmahlzeit

Frühstück I	DM 4,--
Frühstück II (mit Käse, Wurst, Ei)	DM 6,20
Mittagessen oder warmes Abendessen	DM 8,40
Kaffeegedeck	DM 4,40
kaltes Abendessen oder Wanderverpflegung	DM 7,--

Sonderleistungen in der Verpflegung sind nach Absprache mit der Heimleitung und gegen Berechnung möglich.

2. Übernachtungsgebühr

Alle Preise beinhalten fl. Kalt- und Warmwasser und Dusche (Waschgelegenheit und Dusche im Zimmer), Bettwäsche und Hallenbadbenutzung.

4-Bettzimmer	DM 11,70
2-Bettzimmer	DM 15,50
1-Bettzimmer	DM 23,20

Abendliche Schließzeit 23.30 Uhr.

Jetzt bist du dran! 💬

Working with a partner, conduct the following conversation. You/your partner assumes the role of a German person who inquires about your last holiday. Your questions could include the following:

a) Where did you go?

b) When did you go?

c) Did you go alone or with other people?

d) How did you travel?

e) Where did you stay and for how long?

f) What did you do (during the day? in the evening?)

g) What was the weather like?

h) What are your plans for next year?

POST UND BANK

In this unit you will practise:
▷ asking for change,
▶ using a public telephone,
▷ buying stamps for letters, cards and parcels,
▶ sending a telegram,
▷ cashing traveller's cheques and changing currency.

A. Die Post

Hör zu! ❶

You have joined a long queue in a German post office in order to buy some stamps for your letter home. Listen to what the people in front of you say. Whenever your teacher stops the tape, make a note of the following points for each dialogue:

a) how many and what kind of stamps the customer asks for,
b) the cost of each different type of stamp,
c) what the customer has to pay in the end.

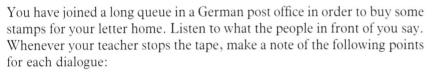

Jetzt bist du dran! 💬

Look at the illustrations below. Working in pairs, enact a roleplay with your partner where you come into the post office and wish to buy stamps for the items in the pictures. Your partner takes the role of the post office clerk.

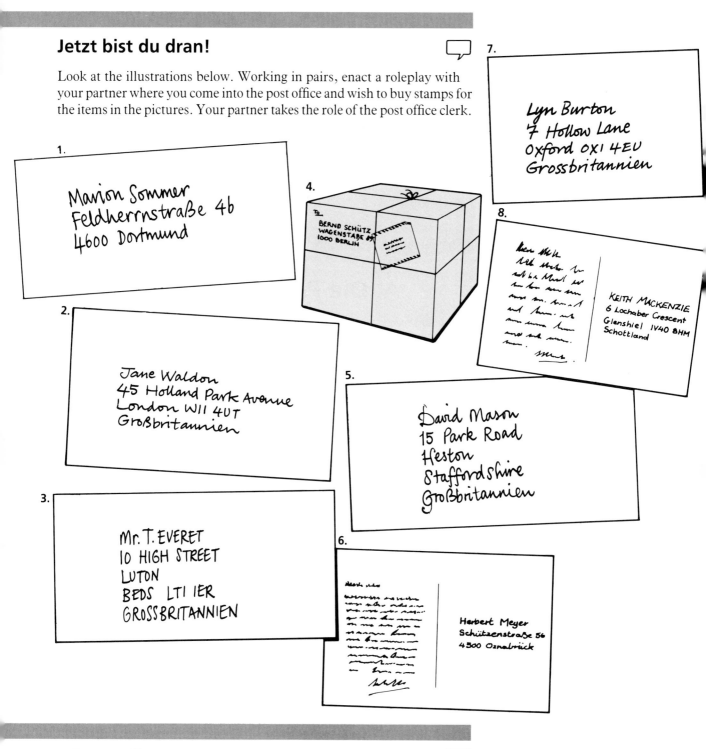

1.
Marion Sommer
Feldherrnstraße 4b
4600 Dortmund

2.
Jane Waldon
45 Holland Park Avenue
London W11 4UT
Großbritannien

3.
Mr. T. EVERET
10 HIGH STREET
LUTON
BEDS LT1 1ER
GROSSBRITANNIEN

4.
TO
BERND SCHÜTZ
WAGENSTABE
1000 BERLIN

5.
David Mason
15 Park Road
Heston
Staffordshire
Großbritannien

6.
Herbert Meyer
Schützenstraße 56
4500 Osnabrück

7.
Lyn Burton
7 Hollow Lane
Oxford OX1 4EU
Grossbritannien

8.
KEITH MACKENZIE
6 Lochaber Crescent
Glenshiel IV40 8HM
Schottland

Hör zu! ❷

A You are waiting for a telephone booth in a German post office to become vacant. The people in front of you seem to be having some trouble finding the right change to phone. Listen to their attempts at changing money with another customer. Note down for each customer:

a) the name of the coin he/she wants to change,

b) whether he/she receives change and if so, exactly which coins he/she receives in exchange.

B Listen to the conversations again. Note how people ask for change in German:

Haben Sie . . . klein?
Hätten Sie vielleicht . . . ?
Können Sie . . . wechseln?

and how they say that they have not got any change either:

Tut mir leid. Ich habe kein Kleingeld.

Hör zu! ❸

A You will hear five conversations in which people try to find out telephone numbers. Listen carefully. Write down in your notebook:

a) the name of the town in which the person they wish to ring lives,

b) the full phone number they obtain.

B Listen to the conversations again. Pick out, and write down, the German for the following:

a) telephone directory,

b) code,

c) just a moment,

d) goodbye,

e) international enquiries.

Jetzt bist du dran!

You are trying to phone home while you are on holiday in Germany. You have various difficulties to overcome. Your partner will do his best to help you.

1. You: Ask someone for change because you only have a 10 Mark note.
Your partner: Ask him/her what sort of change he/she would like.
You: Say you'd like a 5 Mark piece and five single Marks.
Your partner: It appears you only have three 2 Mark pieces and four single Marks.
You: Say that would be O.K.
Your partner: Hand over the money.
You: Thank him/her.

2. You: You don't know the code from Germany. Phone International Enquiries.
Your partner: Auslands-Auskunft.
You: Explain that you need the code for your town in England.
Your partner: Können Sie das wiederholen?
You: Repeat it.
Your partner: Augenblick bitte. Die Vorwahl ist 00 44, gefolgt von der Vorwahl der Stadt, die Sie anrufen, aber ohne die Null vorweg.
You: Thank the operator.

Dienstleistungen

Look at the following advertisements for a number of German banks. Read them carefully, then answer the questions on the top of the next page.

a

Wir sind in Ihrer Nähe

und in allen Geldangelegenheiten zu Hause. Besuchen Sie uns. Machen Sie Gebrauch von unserem Giro-, Spar-, Kredit- und Geldanlege-Service. Und auch Sie werden feststellen:

Kreissparkasse
Bernkastel-Wittlich

Öffnungszeiten unserer
Zweigstelle Piesport

Mo.-Fr.   8.00 - 12.00 Uhr
          13.30 - 16.30 Uhr
Samstag   9.00 - 12.00 Uhr

Mittwoch nachmittag geschlossen

b

Bargeld rund um die Uhr.

Kommen Sie mit Ihrer eurocheque-Karte zu unseren ec-Geldausgabe-Automaten:

- Marienplatz
- Isartorplatz
- Am Harras
- Leopoldstraße 74
- Rotkreuzplatz
- Ostbahnhof, Orleansplatz 3
- Kaufhaus Hertie, Bahnhofplatz*
- Kardinal-Faulhaber-Straße 14*
- zentrum (OEZ)*
- Olympia-Einkaufs-
- Perlach-Einkauf-Passagen (PEP)*

* nur während der Öffnungs- bzw. Schalterzeiten

BAYERISCHE VEREINSBANK

5/18

c

Tag und Nacht für Sie geöffnet.

Abends, 19.30 Uhr. Sie wollen ausgehen und stellen fest, daß Sie nicht genügend Bargeld haben. Was nun? Für diesen nicht gerade seltenen Fall haben wir einen besonderen Service für Sie: den Geldautomaten.

Er ist immer für Sie da. Tag und Nacht. Auch am Wochenende.

KSN mit Geldautomaten
Bargeld rund um die Uhr

d

CHANGE
TRAVELLER CHEQUES
GOLD- UND SILBERMÜNZEN

H+G BANK

Für Geldwechsel auch samstags morgens geöffnet.
Hauptstraße 46 und 208
Stadtplan E 4 · ☎ 26065

e

Wenn's um Geld geht...

S P A R K A S S E

Kreissparkasse
Bernkastel-Wittlich

Trittenheim, Moselweinstraße 44 - Telefon 06507/2515

Unsere Öffnungszeiten:

Montag bis Freitag
  8.00 Uhr bis 12.00 Uhr und
  13.30 Uhr bis 16.30 Uhr

Kapiert?

1. Which of the advertisements refer to service-tills?
2. Which of the advertisements refer to banks?
3. Which of the banks does not open on a Saturday?
4. Which of the banks does not open on a Wednesday afternoon?
5. What differences can you find between advertisements 1 and 5?

B. Die Bank

Hör zu! ❹

A You will hear some conversations which take place in a bank.
Listen to the first two dialogues. Copy the grid below into your
notebook and fill it in.

	wants to change	has to go to counter	anything to sign?	identifi-cation needed	gets how much?
customer 1 customer 2					

B Listen to the two conversations again. Write down the German
expressions for the following:
a) traveller's cheque   d) to sign   g) to change
b) to cash   e) receipt   h) exchange rate
c) foreign desk   f) cash desk

C Now listen to the third dialogue. Explain what transaction has taken
place.

Jetzt bist du dran!

Carry out the following roleplay with your partner:

You have gone to the bank in order to get some cash.

You: Ask which desk you have to go to in order to
            a) cash a traveller's cheque
OR   b) change £40.
Bank clerk: Gehen Sie bitte zum Schalter 4.
You: Tell the clerk there what you want.
Bank clerk: If a) Ihre Unterschrift bitte.
            If b) So, bitte schön.
You: Ask what the exchange rate is.
Bank clerk: Für das Pfund bekommen Sie DM 2,99. Gehen Sie bitte an die
            Kasse.
You: Thank him/her.

FREIZEIT

In this unit you will practise:

▷ talking about your hobbies and activities,

▶ expressing a preference on radio and television programmes,

▷ expressing musical preferences,

▶ arranging to go to the cinema,

▷ arranging to go to the theatre.

A. **Was machst du in deiner Freizeit?**

Hör zu! ❶

A Listen to some young German people talking about what they like doing in their spare time. Write down in your notebook what each speaker's leisure time activities are.

B Listen to the recording again. For each speaker, write down at least one of the activities mentioned in German.

Jetzt bist du dran!

You are having a conversation with your penpal (your partner will play this role) about his/her hobbies. Ask him/her:

1. was er/sie gern in seiner/ihrer Freizeit macht,

2. seit wann er/sie das macht,

3. wie oft er/sie das macht,

4. wo er/sie das macht,

5. wann er/sie das macht,

6. ob er/sie noch andere Hobbys hat.

Write all the answers down in your notebook, because you will have to tell your parents (the class) afterwards what your penfriend likes doing in his/her spare time.

Here are some suggestions for the answers:

1. Ich spiele gern Schach/Fußball/Klavier.
   Ich sammle gern Briefmarken/Münzen.
   Ich stricke/koche/bastle gern.

2. Das mache ich seit einer Woche/drei Monaten/zwei Jahren.

3. Ich mache das einmal/zweimal/viermal in der Woche/im Monat.
4. Ich mache das in der Schule/zu Hause/im Freibad/am See/in der Turnhalle/im Verein.
5. Ich mache das jeden Montag/jeden Dienstagnachmittag/jeden Mittwochabend/am Wochenende/jeden Tag.
6. Außerdem mache ich Krafttraining.
   Ich spiele auch gern Tennis.

Jetzt schreibst du!

Write a letter to your penfriend in Germany about your favourite leisure time activities.

OR

Write a short paragraph about your penfriend's hobbies, based on the conversation you had with him/her.

Was macht man hier während der Freizeit?

Some free time activities. Look at them carefully.
Can you tell what activity each of the notices refers to?

1. KINO-PROGRAMM

2. Ausgabe von Anglererlaubniskarten nur während der Geschäftszeit, an Sonn- und Feiertagen, von 10–11 Uhr

3. Betreten des Schwimmbades nur ohne Schuhe

   Schwimmbadbenutzung nur mit Badehaube

4. Cafe Dachsbau
   Jugendherberge
   Wandergebiet Radberg
   Bitte Unterführung benutzen

5. STARTRAUM HEISSLUFTBALLONS
   RAUM WIRD NACH DEM START GEGEN 16.00 UHR FÜR ZU- SCHAUER FREIGEGEBEN

Kannst du einen passenden Brieffreund finden?

During your stay in Germany, you read the following advertisements in a youth magazine. Read each one of them carefully. Which one do you think you would like to reply to? Say why.

Persönliches

(a) **Berufsschüler,** 16 J., sucht Brieffreundin in England od. Frankreich. Meine Hobbys sind Tanzen, Schwimmen und Popmusik. Schreib mal. Foto bitte! Nassestr. 20, 5 Köln 41

(b) **Schreib mir mal!** Ich bin 15-jährige Realschülerin aus Wien. Hätte gern Brieffreund, Nähe Hamburg. Disko! Zelten! Wassersport! Komm mal zu Besuch. Erwarte Deinen Brief an 1015 Wien, Fach 198 I.H. Kennwort: Wasserratte.

(c) **Silvia,** 14, dunkelhaarig und sportlich. Meine Hobbys sind Tennis, Reisen und klassische Musik. Möchte Brieffreundin in Großbritannien. Näheres unter "Nr. 401.245" an Postfach 389/3100 St Pölten.

(d) **Ulrich,** 15 J., nicht sehr sportlich; bastle gerne – Modellbau – höre gern Musik und spiele Klavier und Querflöte, tanze auch gern. Suche Brieffreundin in England. Schreib mal. Postfach 200211, 3380 Goslar.

(e) Sammler sucht Brieffreund(in) in England. Sammle Postkarten. Schreibe aber auch gern. Andere Hobbys: Lesen, Wandern, Reisen. **Günter** Vollbracht, Alter Zoll 28, 2090 Winsen.

(f) Möchtest Du mein Brieffreund sein? Bin 15 Jahre, Schülerin. Meine Hobbys sind Malen, Puppen basteln, Joggen, Jazz-Gymnastik und Skifahren. Richte Deinen Brief an **Jutta** Köster, Postfach 7454, 8480 Weiden.

Jetzt schreibst du!

A Pick out the person with whom you think you have the most things in common. Write him/her a short letter:

  a) tell him/her how old you are, where you live and which school you go to,

  b) tell him/her about your hobbies, how long you have been doing them, how often, when and where,

  c) ask three questions about hobbies.

B You find that none of these people would really suit you as a penfriend. So you decide to advertise yourself. Write your own advertisement, giving similar details to the ones in the adverts you have just read.

B. Radio und Fernsehen

Hör zu!

You will hear some people talking about radio and television programmes. Listen carefully. Whenever your teacher stops the tape, write down the following information for each case:

a) the programme that is mentioned,

b) the channel,   d) the time it starts,

c) the day it is on,   e) the time it finishes.

Fernsehprogramme

You are in the TV room of the youth hostel in Hamburg. Your friends notice that you are reading the television page in the newspaper, and ask about programmes that interest them. Can you help? Tell them what station the programme is on, when it starts and when it finishes. The questions are on the next page.

SAMSTAG

10.00 heute
10.03 „scheibnerweise"
10.50 Aspekte
11.30 Presseschau
11.35 heute
11.50 ● Programm-Änderung ●
Die Diebe von Marshan, Spielfilm von 1951, mit Tony Curtis
13.15 Vorschau
13.45 Reisewege zur Kunst
14.30 Sesamstraße
15.00 Der Komödienstadel: „Die Widerspenstigen"
16.30 Das Krankenhaus am Rande der Stadt: Die neue Ärztin
17.30 Hier und Heute unterwegs
18.00 Tagesschau, Sportschau
19.00 Markt: 1. **Teure Reparaturen – wer verdient am Service? 2. Geschäfte mit Festen – jeder zweite Tag ein Geschenktag**
19.25 Tanzschule Kaiser Mengenrabatt
20.00 Tagesschau
20.15 Zum Blauen Bock, mit Heinz Schenk und dem Dortmunder Opernsänger Günter Wewel
21.45 Lottozahlen, Tagesschau, Das Wort zum Sonntag
22.05 Wie ein Schrei im Wind, englischer Spielfilm, 1965, mit Oliver Reed und Rita Tushingham
23.50 Revue im Alcazar, von und mit Jean-Marie Rivière
0.50 Tagesschau

11.00 Vorschau
11.30 Mikroprozessor
12.00 Nachbarn in Europa
14.00 Diese Woche
14.20 Damals: Die letzte Kriegs-Wweihnacht
14.30 Wir stellen uns: ZDF-Programmdirektor Alois Schardt
15.00 Elton John (stereo): Rocket-Man und Brillen-Fan, Film
15.45 Es leuchten die Sterne, deutscher Spielfilm von 1938, mit Lil Dagover, Paul Hörbiger und Theo Lingen
17.06 Der Graureiher
17.19 Aktion Sorgenkind berichtet, Der große Preis, Wochengewinner
17.25 heute
17.30 Länderspiegel
18.25 Polizeiarzt Simon Lark: Der Hausgast
19.00 heute

19.30 Die Pyramide
Mit Dieter Thomas Heck
20.15 Jack Lemmon: Nie wieder New York, US-Spielfilm von 1969
21.50 heute
21.55 Das aktuelle Sport-Studio, mit Doris Papperitz
23.10 heute
23.15 Rockpop Music Hall (stereo) mit Talk Talk, Spandau Ballet, Blancmange, Al Corley, Roger Chapman und Dave Edmunds (bis ca. 1.45)

19.00 Aktuelle Stunde
20.00 Tagesschau
20.15 Die 6 von der „Weltreise": Abenteuer im Rückblick
21.15 Einige Blicke auf Meret Oppenheim – Porträt einer Künstlerin
22.15 Vor 40 Jahren: Deutsche Wochenschau
22.45 Made in Sweden, mit Sylvia Vrethammar
23.30 Literatur in Kreienhoop (1): Alfred Paul Schmidt
0.05 Letzte Nachrichten

SONNTAG

9.30 Vorschau
10.00 Weltumsegelung mit Familie
10.45 Die kleine Meerjungfrau
11.15 Die Erde, der Himmel und die Dinge dazwischen (2)
12.00 Internationaler Frühschoppen **Unser Land, welch ein Land? Die Bundesrepublik im Urteil kommender und gehender Korrespondeten**
12.45 Tagesschau mit Wochenspiegel
13.15 Svjatoslav Richter spielt Franz Schubert
13.45 Magazin der Woche
14.30 Peter und der Wolf
15.00 Das Jahr ohne Vater US-Spielfilm, 1972
16.45 Kennen Sie Kino?
17.30 Regenbogen
18.00 ARD-Ratgeber: Recht
18.40 Tagesschau
18.43 Die Sportschau
19.20 Weltspiegel
20.00 Tagesschau
20.15 Adventssingen
20.20 Schwarz Rot Gold: Um Knopf und Kragen, von Dieter Meichsner
22.20 Tagesschau
22.25 Deutsches aus der anderen Republik

23.10 Der Schauspieldirektor Komödie mit Musik von Wolfgang Amadeus Mozart Aufzeichnung aus dem Schönbrunner Schloßtheater, Wien
0.25 Tagesschau

9.50 Vorschau
10.20 Und sie folgten dem Stern (1)
11.30 Mosaik
12.00 Das Sonntagskonzert
12.45 heute
12.47 Sonntagsgespräch
13.15 Die Welt im Tanz
13.45 Morgen schon
11. Ein Mittag mit Pannen
14.15 Alice im Wunderland
14.40 1 – 2 oder 3 Ratespiel mit Michael Schanze
15.35 Rasmus und der Vagabund
16.05 Ein-Blick Zauberpater Pater Lennartz tingelt für ein Jugendheim
16.20 Das Traumschiff
17.20 heute
17.22 Die Sport-Reportage
18.05 Der Windsbacher Knabenchor singt zum Advent
18.15 Katholisches Tagebuch
18.30 Die Muppets-Show
19.00 heute
19.10 Bonner Perspektiven
19.30 Menschenskinder! Der letzte Revolverheld von Wyoming
20.00 Programm-Vorschau
20.15 Bambi '84 Gala-Abend aus dem Deutschen Theater München
22.15 heute Sport am Sonntag
22.30 Moskaus Drang nach Süden 2. Rivalen am Pazifik
23.20 Die fünf Geächteten US-Spielfilm, 1967, mit James Garner
1.00 heute

wdr
Westdeutsches Fernsehen
DRITTES PROGRAMM

19.00 Aktuelle Stunde „Sport im Westen"
20.00 Tagesschau
20.15 Lodynski's Orfeum (1): Eine kabarettistisch-satirische Revue
21.00 Kulturmacher (1): Der Medienmacher Josef Ferenczy
21.45 Adams Apfel: Der Schweizer Physiker und Philosoph Max Thuerknauf
22.30 One world – one peace Sara Vaughan singt Lyrik von Johannes Paul II.
23.15 Literatur in Kreienhoop (2)
0.00 Letzte Nachrichten

Ausführliches Programm in „prisma"

Your friends ask:

1. I can't understand these German programmes. Is there an English film on this weekend?
2. I'd like to see a programme about politics.
3. I would like to see a rock or pop music programme.
4. There must be some sport!
5. When is the news on?
6. All these films are dubbed. Are there any real German films on this weekend?
7. Is there a programme from or about the GDR?
8. Someone said there was an American film on TV this weekend.

Jetzt bist du dran!

Your penfriend is on the coach with you on the way to spending two weeks at your home. You get into a conversation about TV. Act out a roleplay with your partner, talking on the following themes:

Fernsehapparat
— Wo?
— Schwarz-weiß?
— Farbfernseher?

Videogerät?

Lieblingssendung
— Wann?
— Welches Programm?
— Um wieviel Uhr?

Radioprogramme

Pick out a few things you are interested in from the list of programmes on the next page. Find out the starting and finishing times of the programmes you could listen to and write them down in your notebook:

thrillers	news	entertainment
sports programmes	pop music	music from France
classical music	current affairs	
music quiz	weather forecast	

SA
4. Mai

Hörfunk

WDR 3
11.05 Uhr

Krimi in zwei Teilen: „Die Whisky-Killer"

Mit seinem „Krimi am Samstag" führt der WDR die Hörer diesmal (heute und am nächsten Wochenende) auf alkoholische Pfade. Die „Whisky-Killer" in Roderick Wilkinsons gleichnamigem Thriller sind eine Räuber-Bande, die seit Jahren auf einsamer Strecke ganze Transporte mit Ladungen dieses Getränks erbeutet. Die schottische Polizei ist machtlos. Argwöhnisch beäugt sie den kanadischen Privatdetektiv Kenneth Daly, den Chef-Brenner Henry Callingway als letzte Rettung engagiert hat. Daly hat zwar Erfolg bei einer hilfreichen schottischen Schönen, kann aber weder weitere Überfälle noch einen Mord verhindern. Bis er schließlich selbst in die Fänge der Whisky-Bande gerät . . .

Privatdetektiv Daly (gesprochen von Erich Hallhuber, l.) ist die letzte Rettung für den Whisky-Fabrikanten Callingway (Hans Caninenberg)

WDR 1

⬤⬤ Vorwiegend Stereoprogramme

4.30 RADIOWECKER
Frühprogramm (WDR)
5.00 Nachr., Wetter
5.55 Ansage, Choral
6.00 Nachr., Wetter
6.05 Morgenmelodie
6.30 Wetterbericht
6.55 Morgenandacht
Ansprache: Pastor Ulrich Betz, Hamburg
7.00 Nachr., Wetter
7.05 Zeitfunk
Aktuelle Informationen und Meinungen
7.20 Morgenmelodie
7.30 Wetter; Polleninformationsdienst
8.00 Nachr., Wetter
8.05 Deutsche Presse
8.12 Morgenmelodie
8.30 Wetter; Polleninformationsdienst
9.00 Nachr., Wetter
9.05 ERLEBTE GESCHICHTEN
„Dritte Welt aus erster Hand":
Die Iranerin Schohreh erzählt von ihrer Flucht aus der Heimat
Aufgezeichnet von Annlie Hillmer
9.30 Improvisationen mit Musik: **Offene Stimmungen** (4)
Mit Dieter Szametat
10.00 Nachr., Wetter
10.05 Echo West (I)
11.00 Nachr., Wetter
11.05 Echo West (II)
Darin: 11.30 Das Land um halb zwölf
Nachrichten, Berichte und Kommentare
11.45 Landreport
12.00 Nachr., Wetter
12.05 ZWISCHEN BROADWAY UND KUDAMM
Dressed to kill, aus dem gleichnamigen Film (Donaggio). I'm like a fish out of water, aus dem Film „Hollywood hotel" (Whiting). Duel at Diablo, aus dem gleichnamigen Film (Hefti). Schwarzer Walzer, aus dem Film „Morddrohung" (Duval). Susannas Melodie, aus dem Film „Der Neue" (Böttcher). Break, aus dem Film „Spuren eines Unsichtbaren" (Duval). Strawberry woman, The honeyman, Crab man — Bess, you is my woman now — Summertime, aus der Oper „Porgy and Bess" (Gershwin). Indiscreet, aus dem gleichnamigen Film (van Heusen). Titine — Smile, aus dem Film „Modern times" (Bertai/Chaplin). Tear me up — Passion play, aus dem Film „Nachts werden Träume wahr" (Kozinski/Faltermeyer). Frag nicht, warum ich gehe, aus dem Film

„Das Lied ist aus" (Stolz). Just one of those things, aus dem Film „Young at heart" (Porter). Collage aus dem Film „Nachts werden Träume wahr" (Faltermeyer)
13.00 Nachr., Wetter
13.10 Zeitfunk
Darin: Internationale Pressestimmen
13.30 ROTLICHT
Rock-Regal und Ohr-Clip:

Mütter und Töchter

Moderation: Günther Janssen
15.00 SPORT UND MUSIK
Tore — Punkte — Meisterschaft
Fußball-Bundesliga — 29. Spieltag
1. FC Köln — Hamburger SV / SV Waldhof-Mannheim — Eintracht Frankfurt / Borussia Dortmund / Fortuna Düsseldorf / Arminia Bielefeld — Karlsruher SC / SV Werder Bremen — Bayer 04 Leverkusen / FC Bayern München — Borussia Mönchengladbach / VfB Stuttgart — FC Schalke 04
Dazu: Aktuelle Sportnachrichten
18.00 Nachr., Wetter
18.05 Neue Jazzplatten
Vorgestellt von Dietrich Schulz-Köhn
18.30 Echo des Tages
19.00 Nachr., Wetter
19.05 GEDANKEN ZUR ZEIT
Atomisierung der Bilder
Vom Großkino zum Satellitenfenster
Von Wolfram Schütte
19.20 DAS MUSIKRÄTSEL
Ein Quiz London — Köln
Mit Ulrich Dibelius, Peter Heyworth, Karl-Heinz Wocker und — als Leiter der Sendung — Wolfgang Seifert
Thema des Abends:
Im Garten
20.15 TANZPARTY IM WDR
Mit Siw Inger, Ingrid Peters, Volker Lechtenbrink, Timothy Touchton und der WDR Big Band unter Leitung von Werner Müller
Durch das Programm führen Petra Nova und Peter Wolff
(Übertragung aus dem Saalbau in Bottrop)
22.00 Nachr., Wetter
22.05 Kritische Chronik
Aus Politik und Kultur
22.30 BIS DREI DABEI
Nachtprogramm (SWF)
23.00 Nachr., Wetter
23.05 BIS DREI DABEI
Nachtprogramm (SWF)
24.00 Nachr., Wetter
0.05-5.55 DAS ARD-NACHTPROGRAMM
Heute vom SWF
Darin: stündlich Nachr.

WDR 2

4.30 RADIOWECKER
Frühprogramm (WDR)
5.00 Nachr., Wetter
5.55 Morgenandacht
Ansprache: Pastor Ulrich Betz, Hamburg
6.00 Nachr., Verkehr
6.05 Morgenmagazin
Darin: 6.30, 7.00, 7.30, 8.00, 8.30 Nachrichten, Wetter, Verkehr
9.00 Nachr., Verkehr
9.05 ZeitZeichen
4. Mai 1950:
Eröffnung des englischen Kulturinstituts „Die Brücke" in Köln
9.20 Freie Fahrt ins Wochenend
Verkehr, Reise, Freizeit / Pop international
10.00 Nachr., Verkehr
10.05 Freie Fahrt ins Wochenend
Verkehr, Reise, Freizeit / Pop international
11.00 Nachr., Verkehr
11.05 FREIE FAHRT INS WOCHENEND
Verkehr, Reise, Freizeit / Pop international mit Flashback
12.00 Nachr., Verkehr
12.05 Mittagmagazin
Aus aller Welt
Darin: 13.00, 14.00 Nachr., Verkehr
14.45 Klingende Münze
15.00 Nachr., Verkehr
15.05 Treffpunkt
16.00 Nachr., Verkehr
16.05 Unterhaltung am Wochenende
Ein Programm ohne Programm mit Hans Marquardt, Else Stratmann, den „Vier vor 5", Chansons und Szenen
Produktion: Hilmar Bachor
17.00 Nachr., Verkehr
18.00 Nachr., Verkehr
18.05 Hörer machen Programm
19.00 Nachr., Verkehr
20.00 Nachr., Verkehr
20.05 Sportnachrichten
20.10 POP SESSION Plattenbude
Am Mikrofon: Gregor König
21.00 Nachr., Verkehr
21.04 Disco France
Chansons aus Frankreich
Vorgestellt von France Briaut
22.00 Nachr., Verkehr
22.05 SPIELFLECK
Aus Valentins Zeit (5)
Steilwandfahrer / Radlerpech / Die Uhr von Löwe / Die gestrige Zeitung
Von Karl Valentin
Musik: Rudi Knabel
Mit Karl Valentin und Liesl Karlstadt
22.30 MUSIC UNLIMITED
Musik von Orexis, Jasper van't Hof, Chris Doran, Trilok Gurtu und anderen
23.00 Nachrichten, Wetter, Verkehr
23.05 Music unlimited
24.00 Nachrichten, Wetter, Verkehr
0.05 BIS DREI DABEI
Das Nachtprogramm der ARD vom Südwestfunk
Darin: 1.00, 2.00, 3.00 Nachrichten, Wetter
3.05-5.59 Musik bis zum frühen Morgen
Das Nachtprogramm der ARD vom Südwestfunk
Darin: 4.00, 5.00 Nachrichten, Wetter

WDR 3

6.00 Nachr., Wetter
6.05 Konzert
Weber, Krommer, Glinka und Mozart
6.45 Landfunk
6.57 Wasserstände
7.00 Nachr., Wetter
7.05 DAS MOSAIK (I)
C. Stamitz, Haydn, Paganini, Druschetzky
8.00 Nachr., Wetter
8.05 Das Mosaik (II)
Musik der Völker, Berichte und Meinungen aus der Kultur
8.50 Choral
„Was tobet denn der Heiden wilder Hauf" (Unbek. Komponist des 16. Jh.): Singgemeinschaft Bergisch-Gladbach; Ltg. Paul Nitsche
8.55 Morgenandacht
Ansprache: Pastor Ulrich Betz, Hamburg
9.00 Nachr., Wetter
9.05 MUSIK VOM KOMMENTAR BEGLEITET
Histor. Aufnahme
Drei Dirigenten am Pult des Kölner RSO:

Paul Sacher, Eugen Szenkar und Hermann Scherchen
Robert Casadesus, Klavier; Franz-Willy Neugebauer, Trompete
Reger. Serenade für Orchester op. 95. — **Ravel.** Klavierkonzert für die linke Hand. — **Jolivet.** Concertino für Trompete, Streichorch. und Klavier. — **Saint-Saëns.** Sinfonie Nr. 3 c-Moll „Orgelsinfonie"
11.00 Nachr., Wetter
11.05 Krimi am Samstag
Die Whisky-Killer (1)
Von Roderick Wilkinson
Sprecher: Erich Hallhuber, Astrid Jacob, Hans Caninenberg, Jürgen Scheller, Harald Dietl, Hans-Helmut Dickow, Ulf J. Söhmisch, Ute Mora, Bernd Stephan, Horst Johanning, Christoph Lindert, Ekkehard! Belle, Bruno W. Pantel, Henner Quest, Jan Köster, Peter Thom, Karin Gräser. — Regie: Klaus Wirbitzky
12.00 Nachr., Wetter

C. Die Presse

Hör zu! ❸

A number of young German people will tell you which newspapers or magazines they or someone they know like reading. Listen carefully to what they say and note down the following information in each case:

a) the name of the paper or magazine and how often the person reads it,
b) what sort of paper or magazine it is and why it is read.

Pressespiegel

Do you know any of these newspapers or magazines? If so, which?

Jetzt bist du dran!

What sort of papers or magazines does your penfriend read? Ask him/her (your partner will assume this role) in German:

a) Does he/she read the paper every day?

b) If so, which one?

c) And at weekends?

d) What sort of articles does he/she like reading?

e) Which articles does he/she never read?

f) What about magazines?

D. Musik

Hör zu! ❹

A A number of people will tell you about their musical interests. Look at these pictures and match each speaker to the appropriate illustration.

B Once you have listened to the recordings again, note down the instrument played plus one other fact, such as how long or where the speakers practise, whether they like playing or not, etc.

E. Kino und Theater

Gehen wir ins Kino?

You and your friend, who does not speak any German, are on holiday in Vienna and decide to go to the cinema. You pick out two films on the entertainment page of the local newspaper (reproduced on the next page) which look interesting. Can you answer your friend's enquiries?

1. I like detective films. Is either of them a detective film?

2. Am I old enough to be allowed to see *Jenseits von Afrika*?

3. What time is the latest showing of *Müllers Büro*?

4. Can we go on a Sunday?

5. How long has *Müllers Büro* been running?

Jetzt bist du dran!

A You are staying with your German penpal. You have been looking at the entertainment page and your penpal (your partner) is keen to go to the cinema. Work in pairs and conduct a conversation in which you ask the following questions:

a) „Müllers Büro" möchte ich gerne sehen. Wo läuft der Film?

b) Im Karlstor? Wo ist denn das?

c) Neuhauser Straße, das ist doch ganz in der Nähe. Wann ist denn die letzte Vorstellung?

d) Sonntags auch?

e) Was kostet eine Eintrittskarte?

f) Laß uns anrufen und Karten bestellen. Hast du die Telefonnummer?

B Now have a similar conversation with your partner, who will play the role of your penpal. This time, discuss going to see the first showing of *Jenseits von Afrika*.

Gehen wir ins Theater?

Your friend is a keen theatre-goer. Look at these theatre advertisements and answer his/her questions.

1. If I want to make enquiries about what is on at the *Freies Theater München* (FTM), what time should I ring?
2. What time does the performance there start?
3. Are there performances every day?
4. If I want to buy tickets in advance for the *Theater Aporée*, what should I do?
5. I'm interested in the music of the 40s. Can you recommend anything?
6. I just love Shakespeare. Is there anything suitable on? Give as many details as you can.

Schilderwald

Below and overleaf are a number of signs you might come across when following leisure time interests in Germany. Read them carefully. Then answer the question underneath each one:

1. What do you have to observe before you set off here?

2. What does this signpost have to say?

3. What do dog owners have to do in this park?

5. What are people not allowed to do in the *Hofgarten?*

Im Hofgarten ist untersagt:
1. die Wege zu verlassen
2. Rad zu fahren und zu schieben
3. Blumen und Sträucher abzureissen
4. Hunde frei laufenzulassen

Moped-, Radfahren u.
Ballspielen verboten.
Hunde sind an der
Leine zu führen.

Der Gemeindedirektor

4. Where are you not allowed to take your dog or ride your bike?

6. What can you not do here?

STELLPLATZ FÜR
ZWEIRÄDER
BISIKLETLER MOTORSIKLETLER
PARKI

7. What can you do with your bicycles here?

Liebe Kinder, Liebe Eltern!
Kommt herein und schaut euch alles an!
Hier können alle Kinder von 6-14 Jahren
kostenlos bauen, spielen, an Ausflügen
teilnehmen oder unsere Tiere streicheln.
Wir freuen uns auf euren Besuch.

Das BSP-Team

8. What can children between the age of 6 and 14 do in this park?

In this unit you will practise:
▷ discussing what to do on a free day,
▶ making inquiries,
▷ making arrangements.

A. Was machen wir?

Hör zu! ❶

Listen to some people talking about how they intend to spend part of their day. For each conversation write down:
a) what activity they are going to do,
b) why this is thought to be a good idea,
c) where they are going to go.

VIERMASTEN-ZIRKUS **MONTANA**
mit über 100 Tieren und vielen Artisten

Freikarte Gültig nur für die Abendvorstellungen!
bei Erlös einer TIERSCHAUKARTE a. d. Abendkasse

Endlose Möglichkeiten

Read the advertisements for various outings on this and the following page.

Fernsehen ist schön – aber echter Zirkus ist besser

OLYMPIAPARK MÜNCHEN

– Ihr Reiseziel –
Europas größtes Sport- und Freizeitzentrum lädt ein.

Führungen · Besichtigungen · Sport
Freizeit · Spiel · Erholung

Ein Besuch lohnt sich immer:

Ob Sie aus der bayerischen Landeshauptstadt oder seiner näheren Umgebung kommen und Ihnen die Ferien noch bevorstehen, oder ob Sie aus nördlicheren oder südlicheren Gefilden stammen und bereits auf der Rückreise sind.
Den Olympiapark in Ihr Reiseprogramm einzubauen – auch für einen Zwischenstop oder Kurzaufenthalt – das ist das berühmte „Tüpfelchen auf dem i".
Ideale Parkmöglichkeit. Direkte Verkehrsanbindung zur Innenstadt mit U 3 und U 8. |1|5|0|

MÜNCHNER OLYMPIAPARK GMBH
Spiridon-Louis-Ring 21, 8000 München 40
Telefon 0 89/3 06 13-2 04/2 05, Telex 52 80 68 mog d

wander doch mal
Wandern auf sonnigen Almwegen, Sonnenstrahlen blinzeln durch hohe Baumkronen, saftige Wiesen mit Bergblumen säumen den Weg.
Genießer zieht es auf felsige Gipfel. Der See ist immer dabei. Die Brotzeit auf einer Almhütte oder das Entspannen auf einer Sonnenterrasse gehören zum Tegernseer Tal wie die Natur. Erwandern Sie sich's doch mal! |1|4|9|

im tegernseer tal

Informationen: Tegernseer Tal Gemeinschaft
8180 Tegernsee, Tel. 0 80 22 – 39 85
oder bei den Kurämtern
● 8182 Bad Wiessee, Tel. 0 80 22-8 20 51 mit Spielbank
● 8184 Gmund a. T., Tel. 0 80 22-70 55
● 8185 Kreuth, Tel. 0 80 29-10 44
● 8183 Rottach-Egern, Tel. 0 80 22-2 67 40 mit Wallbergbahn
● 8180 Tegernsee, Tel. 0 80 22-3985

Schiffsausflüge auf der Mosel 1989

Koblenz – Cochem – Beilstein
Täglich vom 13. Mai bis 14. Oktober

13.5.–14.10.					13.5.–30.9.	1.10.–14.10.
8.30	ab	Koblenz		an	20.15	18.45
9.10		Moselweiß	r		19.20	17.50
9.30		Winningen	l		19.00	17.30
9.50		Kobern-Gondorf			18.40	17.10
10.45		Alken	r		17.50	16.20
11.00		Brodenbach	r		17.40	16.10
11.30		Moselkern	l		17.10	15.40
12.10		Treis-Karden	r		16.30	15.00
13.15		Cochem			15.55	14.15
14.15	an	Beilstein	r	ab	15.05	—

Trier – Bernkastel-Kues
Täglich vom 13. Mai bis 7. Oktober

9.15	ab	Trier	r	an	19.50 *
10.05		Schweich	l		18.45 *
10.25		Mehring	l		18.25 *
11.45		Trittenheim	l		17.10 *
12.00		Neumagen-Dhron	r		16.55 *
13.25	an	Bernkastel-Kues	r	ab	15.15 *

* – ab 9. September 30 Minuten früher
l – linkes, r – rechtes Moselufer

Preiswerte Moselfahrten

Eine Fülle von Möglichkeiten gibt es da: Zahlreiche Hin- und Rückfahrten mit Landaufenthalten von einer ganzen Reihe von Stationen aus, Nachmittagsausflüge mit Bahnrückreise und vieles mehr. Preiswert! Dafür sorgen z.B. die **verbilligten Rückfahrscheine** mit besonders starker Ermäßigung. Außerdem gibt es Gruppenermäßigung, die bei Schulen sogar 50 % ausmacht. Und Kinder zahlen die Hälfte (bis zu 4 Jahren kostenlos). Auch das Essen und Trinken an Bord ist preiswert und gut.

Der KD-Sparkalender

❋ Jeden Sonn- und Feiertag zahlen Kinder nur DM 3,–. Im Juli und August zusätzlich jeden Dienstag und Donnerstag.
❋ Montag ist Seniorentag, da fahren Senioren zum halben Preis
❋ NEU: Der KD-Seniorenpaß für DM 30,– gilt an allen Tagen
❋ Jeden Samstag, Sonn- und Feiertag ißt die ganze Familie in unserem Bordrestaurant zusammen für nur DM 15,–.
❋ Alle Geburtstagskinder fahren an ihrem Geburtstag zum Nulltarif
Nähere Informationen an den Anlegestellen

Heilbronn ist nicht nur ein Einkaufserlebnis wert. Erleben Sie die Käthchen- und Weinstadt:

Stadtführung (Innenstadtbegehung)
Stadtrundfahrt

Kosten pro Führer: 1. Stunde 35,– DM
jede weitere Stunde: 10,– DM

Viertel(e) nach sechs - die originelle Stadtführung

Die vom 16. April bis 1. Oktober durchgeführten Stadtrundgänge zeigen Ihnen das reizvolle Stadtzentrum mit den interessanten Sehenswürdigkeiten. Nach Abschluß des Rundganges werden Sie von unserem Stadtführer zu einem köstlichen Viertele Heilbronner Wein entführt.

Termine: jeweils Dienstags um Viertel nach sechs
(18.15 Uhr)
16. 4., 30. 4., 14. 5.
28. 5.–3. 9.
wöchentlich
15. 9., 17. 9., 1. 10.
Treffpunkt: Marktplatz vor dem Rathaus
Preis: 5,– DM pro Person für die Führung und ein Viertel Wein
Vorherige Anmeldung nicht erforderlich.

Die Fußgängerzonen laden Einheimische und Gäste zum zwanglosen Bummeln und Verweilen in Straßencafes ein.

Diese Bereiche geben dem Stadtzentrum, südlich und nördlich der Kaiserstraße, eine moderne Note. Heilbronns gutsortierter Einzelhandel strahlt über die Stadt hinaus und weit hinein in den Stuttgarter Raum, ins Hohenloher Land und ins Rhein-Neckar-Gebiet. Optimale Parkmöglichkeiten unterstützen die ideenreichen Bemühungen des Heilbronner Einzelhandels, dessen Jahresumsatz bei einer Milliarde Mark liegt.

A Your host parent (your teacher takes this role) asks you what you would like to do the following day:

Host parent: Wir haben morgen nachmittag frei. Was möchtest du machen,

a) wenn das Wetter schön/schlecht ist?

b) wenn du viel/wenig Geld ausgeben willst?

c) wenn du deine Freunde einladen willst/allein gehen willst?

d) wenn du den ganzen Tag lang weggehen willst?

B Choose one or several possibilities from the advertisements and say why you would like to go there.

Hör zu! ❷

Here are some people talking about how they would like to spend their day.
Write down for each conversation:

a) what is first suggested,

b) whether this suggestion is accepted or not,

c) the reason given,

d) the alternative suggested.

Jetzt bist du dran!

Your exchange partner and you discuss what to do this afternoon. Make a
suggestion. He/she either accepts or declines it. A reason needs to be
given if the suggestion is not taken up!

Start your suggestions with:

| Wir könnten . . . |
| Ich möchte . . . |
| Ich schlage vor, daß . . . |
| Wie wäre es, wenn . . . |
| Wie wär's mit . . . |
| Laß uns doch . . . |
| Hast du Lust, . . . |

Suggestions:	Why not:	Good idea:
Theater	zu müde	eine gute Idee
Tierpark	kein Geld	abgemacht
Fernsehturm	zu anstrengend	das wäre schön
Burgbesichtigung	es regnet	das wäre toll
Dombesichtigung	schlechtes Wetter	das wäre interessant
Stadtrundfahrt	zu windig	das würde Spaß machen
Schlittschuhlaufen	langweilig	prima!
Rheinfahrt	uninteressant	guter Vorschlag
Wanderung	interessiert mich nicht	ja, von mir aus!
Kino	zu teuer	Klasse!

B. Wir rufen vorher an

Hör zu! ❸

Listen to some people phoning up to enquire about various leisure
facilities. Can you complete the missing details below?

1. The swimming pool closes at . . . The last ticket is sold . . .
   You have to . . .

2. Entrance to the zoo costs . . . for children, and . . . for adults, and . . .
   for students. A combination ticket costs . . . for schoolchildren from the
   age of . . .

3. The best way to get to the . . . is by . . . number . . . The stop is . . .

4. It is very difficult to contact . . . by phone as it is closed for . . . and will
   not be open again until . . . It is impossible to visit a museum on . . .

5. Tickets are still available for the performance on . . . The cheapest
   ticket costs . . . It is best to buy the tickets . . .

Jetzt bist du dran!

A Work in pairs. Read the three advertisements on this and the following page carefully. Telephone the locations and ask for three pieces of information (e.g.: Are you open on a Monday? What time do you open/close? Entrance fee? How do you get there?). Your partner will give you the answers according to the information given in the advertisements. The following phrases will help you with your inquiries:

Haben Sie am . . . auf?
Was sind Ihre Öffnungszeiten?
Um wieviel Uhr machen Sie auf/zu?
Was kostet der Eintritt/wie hoch ist der Eintritt?
Was kostet eine Eintrittskarte für Kinder/Erwachsene/Schüler/Studenten?
Wie kommt man am besten dahin?

B Now turn to the individual advertisements again. Answer the questions and complete the exercises for each one.

Kapiert?

Your friend, who is with you on holiday in Germany, is interested in history. Can you help him/her find out details about a visit to the castle?

1. How often do the guided tours take place?
2. How long does a tour last?
3. How do you get to the castle?

Reichsburg Cochem

öffnet ihre Tore vom
1. April bis 30. November
und in der übrigen Zeit
nach Vereinbarung.

Burgführungen

täglich von 9 bis 17 Uhr
jede volle Stunde,
bei Bedarf öfter.

Von Gruppen wird
Voranmeldung erbeten.

Dauer der Burgführung:
40 Minuten

Fußweg Stadtmitte – Burg:
15 Minuten

Burgschänke

täglich von 9 bis 18 Uhr
geöffnet.

Dornröschen-Märchen

Licht- und Tonübertragung
von Ostern bis
1. November, jeweils sonn-
und feiertags nach
Einbruch der Dunkelheit.

Reichsburg GmbH
5590 Cochem, Telefon (02671) 1787 und 3973

Kapiert?

Your exchange partner is going to stay with you in Trier over Christmas. Which of the museums and sites can you visit?

Kapiert?

Tell your friend:

1. The stages of the glass making procedure you can view.

2. The difference between what happens in the *Glasbläserei* and the *Verkauf*.

Auf dem Fluß

While travelling through Germany with your parents, you come across the following signs. Answer the questions your parents have about each sign:

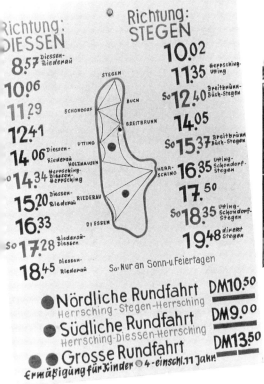

1. Is the journey single or return?

2. How much is the round trip to the south?

4. What kind of boats can we hire here?

3. How long does this trip take?

5. What happens at 8pm here?

Jetzt bist du dran!

A Using the information on this leaflet, act out the following roleplay with your partner:

Suggest to your penpal that, since the weather is so nice, you should go on a trip along the river Mosel tomorrow:

Your friend: Gute Idee. Wo fahren wir denn hin?

You: Suggest a place and a time you should leave.

Your friend: Und um wieviel Uhr kommen wir an?

You: Tell him/her.

Your friend: Ist das nicht etwas zu früh?

You: Suggest then a slightly later boat and say what time it arrives.

Your friend: Und wann fahren wir zurück?

You: Suggest the last boat and tell him/her when it arrives.

Your friend: Prima. Geht in Ordnung.

B Work in pairs:

Your penfriend (your partner) has asked you what you wish to do this afternoon.

You: Suggest to him/her that you go swimming.

Your friend: Warum nicht? Sollen wir zum Agrippabad gehen?

You: Agree and ask him/her how to get there.

Your friend: Wir fahren mit der Bahn. Es ist gar nicht weit von hier?

You: Ask what time the pool closes.

Your friend: Ich glaube um 21.30 Uhr.

You: Ask whether you have to wear a bathing cap.

Your friend: Ja. Das muß man bei uns in allen Bädern.

SUCHEN SIE FREUDE UND ERHOLUNG ?

Möchten Sie einen erholsamen, unvergeßlichen Urlaubstag erleben, so empfehlen wir Ihnen an der beliebten

MOSEL-TAGESFAHRT
von Cochem nach Traben-Trarbach
teilzunehmen.

Die Moselfahrt beginnt um 8.30 Uhr ab Cochem und vermittelt Ihnen in beschaulicher Ruhe herrliche Ausblicke auf die Mosellandschaft. Vorbei an romantischen Burgen und Dörfern wie Beilstein, das „Dornröschen der Mosel", durch den Cochemer Krampen, den Weinorten Ediger-Eller, Bremm, Calmont (höchster Berg der Mosel), Klosterruine Stubben, Alf, Bullay (Marienburg), Weinstadt Zell, Kurstadt Traben-Trarbach mit der Burgruine Gräfinburg.

Zur Stadtbesichtigung ist ausreichend Aufenthalt in Traben-Trarbach gegeben. Rückkunft in Cochem : 19.00 Uhr.

Gute und preiswerte Restauration auf unseren Schiffen.

ab		an
08.30	COCHEM	19.00
08.50	BRUTTIG	18.15
09.30	BEILSTEIN	18.00
09.40	BRIEDERN	17,40
09.50	MESENICH	17.30
	SENHEIM	
10.10	EDIGER	17.20
11.20	ALF	16.35
11.45	ZELL	16.15
11.55	BRIEDEL	16.05
12.05	PÜNDERICH	15.50
12.20	REIL	15.40
12.45	ENKIRCH	15.15
13.15	TR.-TRARBACH	15.00
an		ab

Erste Juni-Woche bis Mitte Oktober jeweils Dienstag, Mittwoch und Donnerstag; Juli und August täglich.

Mosel-Personen-Schiffahrt
Gebr. Kolb
☎ 0 26 71 / 73 87 - ☎ 0 26 73 / 15 15

Öffnungszeiten Hallenbäder	Montag	Dienstag	Mittwoch	Donnerstag	Freitag	Samstag	Sonntag
Agrippabad, Kämmergasse	13.00–21.30	6.30–17.00	6.30–21.30	6.30–17.00	6.30–21.30	8.00–16.00	8.00–12.30
Genovevabad, Berg.-Gladbacher-Str.	13.00–21.30	6.30–17.00	6.30–21.30	6.30–17.00	6.30–21.30	8.00–16.00	8.00–12.30
Hallenbad Bickendorf, Venloer Str.	13.00–17.00	6.30–21.30	6.30–17.00	6.30–21.30	6.30–21.30	8.00–17.00	8.00–12.30
Hallenbad Nippes, Friedrich-Karl-Str.	13.00–17.00	6.30–21.30	6.30–17.00	6.30–21.30	6.30–21.30	8.00–17.00	8.00–12.30
Marsiliusbad, Nikolausstraße	13.00–17.00	6.30–21.30	6.30–17.00	6.30–21.30	6.30–17.00	8.00–17.00	
Hallenbad Chorweiler, Liller Str.	13.00–21.30	6.30–21.30	6.30–21.30	6.30–17.00	6.30–21.30	8.00–17.00	8.00–12.30
Hallenbad Wahn, Albert-Schweitzer-Str.	13.00–21.30	6.30–21.30	6.30–21.30	6.30–18.30	6.30–21.30	8.00–17.00	8.00–12.30
Hallenbad Rodenkirchen, Mainstr.	13.00–17.00	6.30–21.30	6.30–21.30	6.30–17.30	6.30–21.30	8.00–16.00	8.00–12.30
Hallenbad Weiden, Ostlandstr.	13.00–17.00	6.30–21.30	6.30–21.30	6.30–17.00	6.30–21.30	8.00–17.00	8.00–12.30

Jetzt schreibst du!

A These six pictures tell a story. Look closely at them, then write a short story of about 100 words, pretending you are one of the three characters in the pictures.

B Write a letter to your penpal, telling him/her about an outing you had at the weekend. Say:
  a) where you went,
  b) with whom,
  c) what you did,
  d) what the weather was like,
  e) whether or not you enjoyed it.

EINKAUFEN

In this unit you will practise:

▷ what to say in shops,

▶ asking for prices and paying,

▷ making complaints,

▶ reading and understanding advertisements and signs in shops or department stores,

▷ buying petrol.

A. Wo und wann kauft man ein?

Hör zu! ❶

Listen to the conversations on the tape. Where are the speakers going to go shopping? Copy the grid below into your notebook and complete it.

	Name of shop	Item to be bought	Location of shop
1 2 3 etc.			

Was kauft man hier ein?

Look at these photographs. Write down what type of shop you see in each one and what is being sold there.

1.

2.

3.

PARFÜMERIE JOHNEN
INH. H. RECHERMANN

Die neue
Parfümerie
im internationalen
Stil.

am Kirchplatz 1
Tel. 45 44 51

4.

ETAGEN EUROPA MÖBEL

NEU! FLUR- U.
DIELENMÖBEL-ABTEILUNG

Alles Schöne zum Wohnen

5.

LEBENSMITTEL — SUPERMARKT
SCHNELLRESTAURANT
MORITZ u. SENGER

6.

BÜCHERSTUBE

PHONOGERÄTE BÜCHER SCHALLPLATTEN

7.

SCHUH
Schuhe für die ganze Familie

Hör zu! ❷

A Listen to a number of brief conversations in a shop. In each case,

   a) pick out the item asked for from among the pictures on the right,

   b) write down the German name of that item.

B Listen to the recording again. Whenever your teacher stops the tape, note down the German phrase used by

   a) the shopkeeper to ask what the customer wants,

   b) the customer to say what he/she is looking for.

Jetzt bist du dran!

A How would you cope in a shop in Germany? Working in pairs, act out the following roleplays with your partner:

1. Assistant: Kann ich Ihnen helfen?
    You: Say you would like to buy a film.
    Assistant: Möchten Sie einen Schwarzweiß– oder einen Farbfilm?
    You: Say you would like a colour film.
    Assistant: 24 oder 36 Aufnahmen?
    You: Say you want 24 exposures.

2. You: Say you would like a ballpoint pen.
    Assistant: Der hier kostet DM 7 und der hier ist etwas teurer, DM 10,50.
    You: Say you would rather have the DM7 one.
    Assistant: Welche Farbe?
    You: Say which colour you would like.
    Assistant: Das wären DM 7 bitte.
    You: Hand over the money.

3. You: Say you would like some envelopes.
    Assistant: Wieviele möchten Sie?
    You: Say you would like a packet of 20, light blue if they have them.
    Assistant: Es tut mir leid, die haben wir nur in weiß.
    You: Say that's OK.

B Work in pairs. You have just met your friend in the street and he/she is carrying a lot of shopping. Ask him/her what he/she has bought, where it was bought, how much it cost, etc. (The pictures with "Hör zu! ❷" will give your partner some idea of what he/she might have bought.)

Ask:

1. Was hast du gekauft?
2. Wo hast du es gekauft?
3. Was hat es gekostet?

B. Im Kaufhaus

Hör zu! ❸

You will hear some recordings of people asking the way to various places in a big department store. Listen carefully and note down:

a) the departments asked for,

b) how to get there.

Jetzt bist du dran!

Work in pairs. You have gone shopping in a large department store. Choose one of the departments from the store guides above and ask the shop assistant (your partner) how to get there.

Possible questions:

Entschuldigen Sie bitte, wo ist . . .?
Ich suche die . . . – Abteilung. Wissen Sie, wo die ist?
Können Sie mir sagen, wie ich zur . . . – Abteilung komme?

Possible answers:

Im zweiten/dritten/vierten/usw. Stock.
Neben der . . . – Abteilung im x. Stock.
Im Erdgeschoß, hinter der Musik–/Schreibwaren–/
    Haushaltswarenabteilung, etc.
Auf der x. Etage, rechts/links von der Rolltreppe.

Hör zu! ❹

You will hear some people asking for help with their purchases. In each case, find out:

a) what the item is,

b) what the problem is,

c) the solution.

Was bedeutet das?

What would these signs mean if you saw them in a shop?

Zentralkasse

Aufzug

Notausgang

WC

Rolltreppe

Information

Sonderangebot

Umtausch

Telefon

C. Lebensmittel

Einkaufen

Look at these photographs and answer the question for each one.

1. Was kauft man
   auf dem Markt?

2. Wo kauft
   man Brot?

3. Wo kauft man Fleisch?
4. Wo kauft man Waschpulver?

Hör zu! ❺

Listen to these three conversations and write down what the people are buying and how much it costs.

Jetzt bist du dran!

You are camping in Germany. It is your turn to do the cooking. Go to the market and buy what is required in each of the following situations. Your partner will play the part of the stall holder.

1. You have decided to make a fruit salad.
2. The weather has not been too good, so a nice casserole would be appreciated.
3. What about a crispy salad?

The following phrases might help you:

Assistant:	Customer:
Bitte schön?	Ich hätte gern . . .
Sind Sie dran?	Ich möchte . . .
Werden Sie schon bedient?	Nein danke, das wär's.
Haben Sie noch einen Wunsch?	
Sonst noch etwas?	
Das macht DM . . . zusammen.	

Wieviel?

These weights will help you when you go shopping.

ZWEI KILO

EIN KILO

ZWEI PFUND

EIN HALBES KILO

500 GRAMM

EIN PFUND

250 GRAMM

EIN HALBES PFUND

EIN STÜCK

ZWEI STÜCK

100 GRAMM

Im Lebensmittelgeschäft

So many different kinds of container! Read the text. Decide in what order the illustrated articles appear in the text.

1. Bier, Coca-Cola, Pfirsiche, Spaghetti, Tomaten, Erbsen usw. kann man in einer **Dose** kaufen.
2. Tomatenketchup, Wein und andere Getränke kauft man in einer **Flasche**.
3. Manchmal kauft man Obst, Würstchen oder Fruchtsaft in einem **Glas**.
4. Mayonnaise und Senf kommen in einer **Tube**.
5. Pralinen und Zigaretten kauft man in einer **Schachtel**.
6. Man kauft aber eine **Tafel** Schokolade.
7. Man kauft ein **Stück** Fleisch oder Brot.
8. Chips und Bonbons kauft man in einer **Tüte**.
9. Tomaten und Zwiebeln bekommt man oft in einem **Netz**.
10. Joghurt kauft man in einem **Becher**.
11. Wenn man viel Bier oder Apfelsaft trinkt, ist es billiger, eine **Kiste** zu kaufen.

Hier sieht man auf einen

DER NEUE STÜSSGEN EINFACH FRISCHER!

DER NEUE STÜSSGEN

Jetzt bist du dran!

A You help your penfriend to organise a birthday party. Make out a shopping list for the food and drink you wish to buy and read it out to your friend (your teacher).

B Look at this supermarket advertisement. Work out the cost of the items on your shopping list as far as they are listed.

C Tell your friend (your teacher) which item(s) you could not buy in this particular supermarket and will have to buy elsewhere.

FLEISCH — für Sie vom Metzger frisch vorbereitet!

Frische, dicke Fleischrippe vollfleischig, mager, 1 kg — **7.99**

Schweinerbraten mager, 1 kg — **7.49**

Kasseler Rippenspeer mager goldgelb geräuchert, 1 kg — **9.49**

Rheinischer Sauerbraten fertig eingelegt nach Hausfrauen Art, 1 kg — **9.95**

Frischer Schweinebauch am Stück, 1 kg — **6.49**

I a Lummerkotelett extra magere Spitzenqualität, 1 kg — **8.99**

Frische Bratwurst 1 kg — **7.99**

I a Schweine-Rückensteak extra magere Spitzenqualität, 100 g — **1.59**

Endivien Kl. II Stück — **–.69**

Möhren Kl. II 1-kg-Beutel — **–.69**

Tomaten Kl. II 500-g-Netz — **–.99**

Bananen 1 kg — **1.59**

Speisekartoffeln „Bintje" mehligkochend Kl. I, 5-kg-Beutel — **1.59**

Südafrika Valencia Orangen Kl. I, 10-kg-Netz — **2.99**

TIEFKÜHLKOST

Rahm-spinat gefroren, 600-g-Packung — **1.99**

Erbsen gefroren, 300-g-Packung — **1.49**

10 Fisch-stäbchen gefroren, 300-g-Packung — **1.99**

Dr. Oetker Pizza Salami gefroren, 300-g-Packung — **2.99**

Mc Cain 1-2-3 Frites gefr., 750-g-Beutel — **1.79**

Coppenrath + Wiese Bisquit-Sahne-Rollen gefr., sortiert, 400-g-Packung — **4.79**

KÄSE-THEKE

Cantadou Frischkäse mit Kräutern, Meerrettich oder natur 70% Fett i. Tr., 100 g — **1.99**

Holl. Gouda Pikantje 48% Fett i. Tr., 100 g — **–.99**

Holl. Edamer 40% Fett i. Tr. 100 g — **–.69**

BROT & KUCHEN

Bauernkrone Weizenmischbrot 750-g-Packung — **2.29**

Altdeutsche Bauernschnitten 500-g-Packung — **1.79**

Riesenmarmor-kuchen 600-g-Stück — **2.99**

MIT UNS KÖNNEN

den Vorteils-Kauf
Blick!

DER NEUE STÜSSGEN EINFACH BESSER!

EINFACH BILLIGER!

MOLKEREI-PRODUKTE

vita Fruchtjoghurt
mager
3 x 125-g-Becher
-.89

Müller Knusper-joghurt 3,5% Fett
175-g-Becher
-.69

Tiffany Joghurt
mit Ballaststoffen
3,5% Fett
250-g-Becher
-.79

Elite Pudding
mit Dessertsoße
500-g-Becher
1.99

Müller Kur-Müsli 3,5% Fett
175-g-Becher
-.69

WEIN & SPIRITUOSEN

83er Hecklinger Burg Lichteneck
Q.b.A., 1-l-Flasche
4.99

Eckart Ruländer
Q.b.A., 1-l-Flasche
5.75

Faber Sekt Krönchen
2 x 0,2-l-Packung
3.99

Eierlikör
20 Vol. %
0,7-l-Flasche
6.99

LEBENSMITTEL

Rama
reine Pflanzen-margarine
500-g-Becher
1.69

Kaffee
filterfein gemahlen
500-g-Vac.-Packung
9.79

Nuß-Nougat-Creme
400-g-Glas
1.69

Böklunder Würstchen
10 = 500-g-Glas
3.99

Champignons
III. Wahl – geschn.
370-ml-Glas
1.69

Jetzt Tomaten-Ketchup
600-g-Flasche
1.79

Maggi Flocken-püree 9 Portionen
250-g-Packung
2.69

Maggi Semmelknödel, Rohe Klöße oder Kartoffel-Knödel im Kochbeutel
Packung
2.69

Ital. Pfirsiche
1/2 Frucht
850-ml-Dose
1.49

Silber-zwiebeln
370-ml-Glas
-.99

Hier gibt es, was dem Gaumen Freude macht. Leckere Salate und Spezialitäten, wie's am besten schmeckt. Unsere Fachleute haben an alles gedacht – ob Deftiges, Pikantes oder Kräftiges – Wurst vom appetitlichen Aufschnitt bis zum Katenschinken. Schauen Sie sich mal um, was wir Ihnen zu bieten haben:

Zungenwurst
Fettstufe 25%
100 g
1.29

Schinkenspeck
100 g
1.69

Krusten-schinken
100 g
2.29

Knäckebrot
versch. Sorten
200-g-Packung
-.89

Geschälte Tomaten
850-ml-Dose
-.99

De Beukelaer Prinzenrolle
400-g-Rolle
2.49

Fanny Frisch Chipsfrisch
ungarisch, 175-g-Beutel
2.89

Bahlsen Peppies
75-g-Beutel
1.79

Pfälzer Leber-, Blut- oder Zwiebelleberwurst
Fettstufe 30-35%
100 g
-.99

Geräucherter Bauchspeck
100 g
-.89

Kräuter-sülze
Fettst. 10%, 100 g
-.99

DROGERIE

3-Wetter-Taft
Haarspray, sortiert
300-ml-Dose
2.59

Nur die Supersitz Strumpfhose
Packung
2.25

Tempo Taschen-tücher
6 x 10 Packung
-.99

Servietten
sortiert
20er-Packung
-.99

Geschirr-spülmittel
1-l-Flasche
1.69

SIE RECHNEN!

D. **Kleidung**

Hör zu! ❻

What are these people buying? Copy the grid below into your notebook and complete it.

Item	Size	Material	Design	Price	Taken or not	If not, reason
1. 2. 3. etc.						

Hör zu! ❼

You will hear a number of people who want to change something they have bought, or are wanting their money back. For each person find out:

a) the item in question,

b) how and where they obtained it,

c) what the problem is,

d) what they want the shop to do for them.

Jetzt bist du dran!

You have bought an article of clothing in a shop, but it's not quite right. Go back to the shop and ask the assistant (your partner) if you can change the item, or have your money back.

You should find these phrases helpful:

Er/sie/es ist zu groß/zu klein.

Es hat ein Loch.

Die Farbe paßt nicht.

Er/sie/es ist eingelaufen. Ich bin sehr unzufrieden mit . . .

Hier habe ich meine Quittung.

Ich möchte mein Geld zurück haben.

Ich habe ihn/sie/es als Geschenk bekommen.

E. **An der Tankstelle**

Hör zu! ❽

Listen to the recording. Copy out the grid opposite and, in each case, fill in the amount which has to be paid, tick what else is required, and write in the location where this service can be found.

	Amount	Air/Water/Oil	Location
1. 2. 3. etc.			

Hör zu! ❾

Listen to the recording. Can you match each conversation to one of the symbols below?

a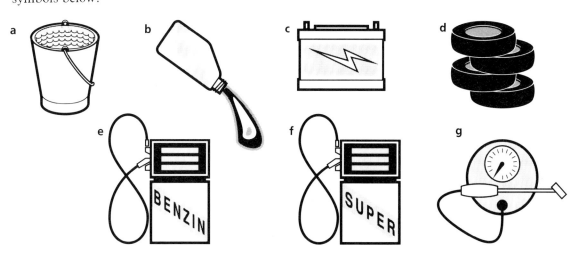

b

c

d

e

f

g

Jetzt bist du dran!

Act out the following roleplay with your partner:

While driving through Germany with your family, you go to a garage and fill up with petrol.

a) Take your voucher (*Beleg*) to the pay desk. Tell the assistant (your partner) which pump you used (*Zapfsäule*).

b) Ask the attendant (your partner) to check (*kontrollieren*) the following:
   den Ölstand,
   den Wasserstand,
   den Reifendruck,
   die Batterie.

ESSEN UND TRINKEN

In this unit you will practise:

▷ reading a menu,
▶ ordering food and drink,
▷ asking for the bill and paying,
▶ what to say at table.

A. Schnellimbiß

Wo kann man in der Stadt schnell essen?

Here are some photographs of places where you can buy fast food and take-aways in Germany. Look at them closely and say what type of food you think you could buy in each place.

3.

KARLSBERG BIER

PIZZERIA

ADRIA

ALLE SPEISEN AUCH ZUM MITNEHMEN

1.

Rindswurst mit Brötchen DM 2.50

Zwiebel Steak DM 7.50

Knoblauch Steak DM 7.50

Mexiko Steak DM 7.50

Kräuterbutter Steak DM 7.50

Rostbratwurst m. Brötchen DM 2.50

IMBISS-GASTSTÄTTE Zum Münzplatz

Schultheis Pilsener

2.

4.

PEPSI

Pommes frites

zum Mitnehmen

5.

Eis zum Mitnehmen

Hörnchen: 0,40 0,80 1,20 usw.

Becher: 0,80 1,20 1,60 usw.

Portion Sahne:

Hör zu! ❶

A You will hear a number of conversations that take place in an
Imbißstube (take away and fast-food bar). Listen carefully. Pick out the
correct order for each customer from the six orders below.

Pommes frites
Mayonnaise

a

Schaschlik
Brötchen

b

Currywurst
Senf

c

Frikadelle mit
        Brötchen
Currywurst mit
        Pommes frites
Pommes frites
        (2×groβe)
Schaschliksoβe
Senf

d

Jägerwurst
Bockwurst
Brötchen
Pommes frites
        (groβe)
Mayonnaise

e

Bratwurst
kleine Pommes frites
Ketchup

f

B When you have listened to the recording again, write down in your
notebook what the customer ordered in each case and what he/she had
to pay.

Jetzt bist du dran!

A Work in pairs. Using the six orders above, reproduce a conversation
similar to the ones you have just heard, with your partner taking either
the role of the customer or the person working in the *Imbißstube*.

B Once you have worked through all the situations, team up with another
pair and work in groups of three or four. One of you assumes the role of
Wurstwart, the others come to buy something at the stall or in the shop.
The picture will help the *Wurstwart* to ask the right questions. Make up
as imaginative an order as possible!

Bitte schön?

Sonst noch
etwas?

Kommt etwas
dazu?

Zum Hieressen
oder zum
Mitnehmen?

B. In der Kneipe

Hör zu! ❷

A Listen to the conversations in which various types of drinks are being ordered. Copy the grid below into your notebook and tick the drinks which are being ordered in each conversation.

B Listen to the recording again. Whenever your teacher stops the tape, write down the quantity that has been ordered, i.e. whether a glass, a cup, a pot, a small or a large glass, or a bottle has been ordered.

Recording:	1	2	3	4	5
Grape juice					
White wine					
Orange juice					
Beer					
Mineral water					
Coffee					
Coca Cola					
Tea					
Chocolate					
Lemonade					
Apple juice					
Red wine					

Hör zu! ❸

A You will hear two conversations in which someone wishes to pay for drinks. Listen carefully and write down for each conversation:
a) the names of the drinks consumed,
b) whether they pay together or separately.

B Listen to the recording again. Write down how the guest says in German that he/she wishes to pay and how the waiter/waitress asks how they want to pay.

Jetzt bist du dran!

A Work in groups of four. One of you takes the leading role and orders drinks for everyone. The drinks list below will be helpful in deciding what you wish to order. Another member of the group plays the waiter/waitress and takes the order down. The illustration will give him/her some idea about what to ask.

B Once you have enjoyed your drink, you wish to pay. Call the waiter/waitress back and tell him/her you want to pay. Is one of you going to pay the entire bill or are you going to pay individually? The waiter may ask you:

Zusammen oder getrennt?

Was hatten Sie denn?

C From the drinks list below, work out how much you will have to pay.

Alkoholfreie Getränke

Pepsi-Cola oder Mirinda	2,60
Mineralwasser	2,60
Bitter Lemon	3,75
Ginger Ale	3,75
1 Glas Zitrone naturelle	4,–
1 Glas Tomatensaft	4,–
Karaffe Apfelsaft (0,2 l)	3,75
Karaffe Johannisbeersaft (0,2 l)	4,25
1 Glas Orangensaft, frisch gepreßt (0,1 l)	4,25

Spirituosen

Kölsch 2/10	2,–
Asbach Uralt 2 cl	4,–
Franz. Cognac, Remy Martin 2 cl	6,–
Fürst Bismarck 2 cl	3,75
Malteserkreuz Aquavit 2 cl	4,–
Aalborg Jubiläums Aquavit 2 cl	5,–
Calvados 2 cl	5,–
Doppelwachholder 2 cl	3,50
Jägermeister 2 cl	4,–
Fernet Branka 2 cl	5,–
Underberg 2 cl	5,–
Kirschlikör 2 cl	4,–
Apricotlikör 2 cl	4,–
Kirschwasser 2 cl	5,–
Williamsbirne 2 cl	5,–
Himbeergeist 2 cl	5,–

Wein, Südwein und Sekt

Karaffe Moselwein Burger Hahnenschrittchen, fruchtig, süffig 0,25 l	6,50
Karaffe Rheinwein Oppenheimer Krötenbrunnen 0,25 l	6,50
Karaffe Weißherbst Badischer Spätburgunder 0,25 l	6,50
Karaffe Rotwein Gau Algesheimer Abtei, trocken 0,25 l	6,50
1 Glas Portwein	4,–
1 Glas Vermouth rot	4,–
1 Glas Vermouth weiß	4,–
M.-Chadon 0.25 l Flasche	9,–
Henkel trocken 0,7 l Flasche	30,–
Fürst Metternich 0,7 l Flasche	32,50
M.-Chadon 0.75 l Flasche	35,–

Kaffee und Kuchen 💬

Look at the photographs. Which cakes would you order? How much would you have to pay?

Hör zu! ❹ 📼

Here are two pages from a waiter's/waitress's notepad. Listen to the recording, and decide which page goes with which order.

Jetzt bist du dran! 💬

A Look at the menu at the top of the page opposite, and tell your teacher what you would like to order from it.

B Work in groups of three or four. Some of you enter a German café and order some cake at the counter. One person plays the assistant who decides which cakes are still available, which cakes are on special offer, which are sold out, etc. Once you have practised ordering cakes, one of you assumes the role of waiter/waitress and takes down your orders for the drinks to go with the cakes. The drinks list and the cake menu reproduced in this section will help you.

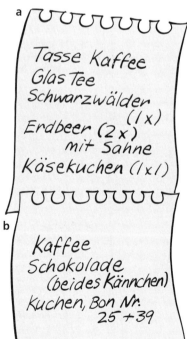

a

Tasse Kaffee
Glas Tee
Schwarzwälder
   (1x)
Erdbeer (2x)
   mit Sahne
Käsekuchen (1x1)

b

Kaffee
Schokolade
   (beides Kännchen)
Kuchen, Bon Nr.
   25 + 39

Kaffeegebäck-Spezialitäten	DM
Cremetorten (siehe Auswahl)	2,40
Sahnetorten (siehe Auswahl)	2,50
Obstkuchen (siehe Auswahl)	2,40
Cremedessert	1,80
Sahnedessert	1,80
Mohrenkopf mit Sahne	2,–
Ananas-Sahnetörtchen	1,80
Wiener Apfelstrudel	1,60
Kirschstreußelschnitten	1,80
Mille-Feules	1,60
Plundergebäck	1,20
Blätterteig	1,20
Nußbeugerl	1,40
Bobbes-Brezel (Olga-Brezel)	1,–
Schillerlocken	2,–
Nußknacker	1,80
Florentiner	1,80
Sahnemeringe	2,20

Café Mohrenköpfle; Inh. Walter Eckhardt
7900 Ulm (Donau), Münsterbazar, Postfach 3026
Tel. (0731) 63703

Ulmer-Spezialitäten-Conditorei am Münster

Eisspezialitäten

You have received this letter from your German penfriend. Read it carefully, then tackle the activity on the next page.

Liebe Eman,

Im Moment ist es furchtbar heiß hier bei uns. Wenn wir doch schon Sommerferien hätten! Ich gehe fast jeden Tag nach der Schule mit ein paar Freunden in die italienische Eisdiele gleich hier um die Ecke. Das Eis dort schmeckt einfach einmalig. Wenn ich knapp bei Kasse bin, kaufe ich nur ein kleines Eis im Hörnchen zum Mitnehmen. Am liebsten mag ich Straciatella und Mocca. Aber ab und zu leiste ich mir einen großen Eisbecher.

Am liebsten mag ich Bananensplit oder Spaghettieis mit viel Sahne. Meine Freundin ißt am liebsten einen Früchtebecher. Wenn wir auf unsere Linie achten wollen, trinken wir manchmal auch nur einen Cappuccino oder einen Espresso.

Gibt es bei Euch auch italienische Eiscafés? Hier gibt es unheimlich viele davon. Der Sommer wäre ohne sie gar nicht denkbar.

Schreib mir doch mal.

Alles Liebe

Elke

Jetzt bist du dran!

A Tell your friend (your partner) about Italian icecream parlours and about the kind of things one can order there. Don't forget to mention that you can get more than just icecream!

UNSERE EISSORTEN

Milch-Speiseeis mit Fettglasur

Vanille	Stracciatella
Schokolade	Pistazien
Malaga	Caramel
Nuß	Zabaglione
Mokka	

Frucht-Speiseeis

Zitrone	Orange
Erdbeer	Heidelbeer
Banane	Himbeer
Ananas	Kirsch
Aprikosen	

Normale Portion Eis	DM 2.50
Große Portion Eis	DM 5.—
Schlagsahne zusätzlich	DM 0.80
Portion Schlagsahne Extra	DM 1.50
Paket Eiswaffeln	DM 1.—

ITAL. EIS-SPEZIALITÄTEN

Coppa Ambassador Vanille-Nuß Eis Brombeerfrucht und Rasberrylikör	DM 8.50
Coppa Italia Milcheis gem. Kirschlikör Sahne	DM 6.50
Fruchtcocktail Milcheis, verschiedene Früchte Cherry Brandy. Sahne. Amarenakirsche	DM 6.50
Coppa Amarena Eis, Amarenakirschen, Amarenasaft, Sahne	DM 6.—
Coppa Amaretto Milcheis gem. Amarettolikör. Sahne	DM 6.50
Coppa Malaga Vanilleeis, Malagawein und Sahne	DM 6.50
Coppa Denise Zabaglione u. Zitroneneis, Himbeeren u. Himbeerlikör Sahne. Cocktailkirsche	DM 7.50
Fruchtbecher Fruchteis, verschiedene Früchte. Curaçaolikör. Sahne. Amarenakirsche	DM 7.50
Coppa Poker Vanille, Carameleis, Aprikosen in Alkohol, Aprikosenlikör. Sahne	DM 10.--
Coppa Patrizia Schokoladeneis, Mandarinen, Eierlikör. Sahne	DM 6.50
Coppa Schwarzwald Milcheis, Sauerkirschen, Schwarzwälder Likör und Sahne	DM 7.—
Coppa Hawaii Zabaglione u. Ananaseis, Ananasfrucht. Likör, Sahne	DM 6.50
Erdbeer Becher (Nur in der Saison) Vanille u. Erdbeeeis, frische Erdbeeren. Sahne	DM 7.—
Spaghetti Eis Vanilleeis, Erdbeersauce. Sahne	DM 6.—
Banane Royal Eine Banane, gem. Eis, Aprikosenlikör. Schokoladenglasur	DM 7.—
Capriccio Becher Vanille u. Mokkaeis, halber Pfirsich. Scotch Whisky. Schokoladensplitter. Curaçaolikör. Sahne	DM 8.—
Spiegelei Milcheis gem. halber Pfirsich, Aprikotlikör	DM 6.50
Cassata Vanille u. Schokoladeneis, Sahnefüllung mit Kandierten Früchten. Mandeln u. Maraschino Likör	DM 5.—
Spumone Sahneeis mit Vanille und Schokoladengeschmack	DM 5.50
Eiskaffee Vanille und Mokkaeis, Schwarzer Kaffee und Sahne	DM 5.—

Eisschokolade Schokoladeneis, Schokoladenmilch und Sahne	DM 5.—
Himbeer Becher Vanille u. Himbeereis. Warme Himbeeren. Sahne	DM 7.—
Coppa Tropical Frucht und Milcheis gem. verschiedene Früchte. Mangos-Kiwi-Ananas-Papaya, Sahne, Cointreau	DM 10.--
Zitronensorbet Zitroneneis mit Sekt	DM 8.—

MILCH-EIS-SHAKE

Vanille - Schokolade - Nuß - Erdbeer - Zitrone oder Banane	DM 3.—

WARME GETRÄNKE

Espresso	DM 2.50
Tasse Kaffee	DM 2.50
Tasse coffeinfreier Kaffee	DM 3.—
Tasse Cappuccino	DM 3.—
Glas Tee mit Zitrone oder Milch ...	DM 2.50
Irish Coffee mit Original Irish Whiskey	DM 7.50
Tasse Schokolade	DM 2.50
Tasse Schokolado mit Sahne	DM 3.—

KALTE GETRÄNKE

Zitronensaft	DM 4.50
Orangensaft	DM 4.50
Himbeersoda 0,2 l.	DM 3.—
Coca Cola 0,2 l.	DM 2.50
Perrier Natürliches Mineralwasser .	DM 3.—
Schweppes Bitter Lemon	DM 3.50

ALKOHOLISCHE GETRÄNKE

Martini Rosso - Bianco	DM 3.50
Martini Dry	DM 4.—
Campari Soda (mit Farbstoff) 4 cl. .	DM 5.50
Pernod 2 cl.	DM 4.50
Mumm Mini	DM 8.—
Ital. Grappa 2 cl.	DM 3.50
Franz. Cognac 2 cl.	DM 4.—
Pils - Bier 0,33 l.	DM 3.50

VERSCHIEDENE TORTEN

Obstkuchen	DM 3.—
Sahnetorten	DM 3.50

ZUM ESSEN

Ital. Toast-Brot	DM 4.50
mit Schinken und Käse	

B You have gone into an Italian icecream parlour with your penfriend (your partner). Read the menu (above) and ask your friend what some of the sundaes are. He/she reads the answer off the menu.

Example:

You: "Coppa Patrizia", was ist denn das?

Your partner: Das ist Schokoladeneis mit Mandarinen, Eislikör und Sahne.

Change roles once you have asked about five different types of icecream sundae on offer.

Besuchen Sie unseren

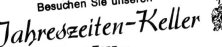

Jahreszeiten-Keller

zum Tanz —
mit internationalen Kapellen

Wir empfehlen Ihnen das

Spätrestaurant

nach dem Theater — Küche bis 2.00 Uhr
Tischbestellung: (040) 34 94 1

Hotel Vier Jahreszeiten

Hamburg 36, Neuer Jungfernstieg 9–14
Geöffnet 21.00 bis 2.00 Uhr außer sonn- und feiertags

Bootshafen-Restaurant

am Forggensee
Füssen, Telefon 08362-7646
Das lohnende Ausflugsziel zu jeder Jahreszeit!
Bekannt gute Küche (warme Küche durchgehend
bis 21.00 Uhr)
Große Sonnenterrasse

Im Sommer täglich Unterhaltungsprogramm:
Folklore — Pop — Wunschkonzert — Bayer. Abende
— Evergreens — Hafenkonzerte
Näheres über Veranstaltungen siehe Kur- und
Tageszeitung.

VEGETARISCHES SPEISEHAUS

montags — freitags 12 – 14 Uhr
Kurfürstenanlage 9 b. Parkhaus
Telefon (06221) 22814

BERNDS KOGGE

Fischspezialitätenrestaurant
lebende Hummern u. Austern

Willkommen an Bord, fragen Sie Bernd,
was die Küche noch bereithält

geöffnet von 18–1 Uhr. Sonntag Ruhetag
Nymphenburger Straße 215 (Ecke Südl. Auf-
fahrtsallee), 8000 München 19. Tel. 16 87 87

Warme Küche bis 24 Uhr

RISTORANTE ITALIANO COMO

(STADT BERGHEIM)

HEIDELBERG
Bergheimer Str. 23
TELEFON 214 13

Italienische,
Jugoslawische und
Fisch-Spezialitäten

Täglich außer Sonntag von 11 bis 24 Uhr — Stadtplan D 4

D. Im Restaurant

Wir gehen essen

Look at the selection of restaurant advertisements on this page. Your
brother/sister/father/mother/friend (your teacher will take this role)
suggests you go out for a meal together. He/she asks you the following
questions. Answer him/her, using the information on the advertisements:

1. Ich möchte Fisch essen. Kennst du ein Restaurant mit Fisch-
   spezialitäten?

2. Ich habe Hunger, aber es ist schon 23.30 Uhr. Welches Restaurant hat
   jetzt noch auf?

3. Ich möchte heute abend ganz gern tanzen gehen. Gibt es ein Restaurant,
   in dem man auch tanzen kann?

4. Es wäre schön, wenn wir beim Abendessen Musik hören könnten.
   Welches Restaurant hat eine Musikkapelle?

5. Kennst du ein vegetarisches Restaurant?

Jetzt bist du dran!

Using the advertisements on page 111, discuss with your partner where you should eat. Act out the following situation:

Your partner: Hast du Lust, heute abend essen zu gehen?
You: Say yes, that is a good idea. Ask what type of food he/she fancies: French, Italian, Chinese?
Your partner: Ich habe Lust auf italienisches Essen.
You: Find a suitable place from the advertisements and suggest going there.
Your partner: Haben die heute auch auf?
You: Check whether they are open today and answer accordingly.
Your partner: Von wann bis wann ist das Restaurant denn auf?
You: Tell him/her the opening hours.
Your partner: Sollten wir vielleicht vorher buchen?
You: Tell him/her whether you think that will be necessary.

Wie und wann ißt man in Wien?

You are going to Vienna with your parents. They find this information in a brochure. Briefly explain to them (your teacher) what it means. How and when can you have breakfast, lunch and dinner in Vienna?

ANMERKUNGEN

Frühstück wird, wenn nicht anders vermerkt, von 8.00 bis 10.00 Uhr serviert und besteht aus Kaffee, Tee oder Kakao, Gebäck, Butter, Marmelade oder Honig (Wiener Frühstück mit Ei). Auf Wunsch wird auch ein amerikanisches bzw. englisches Frühstück serviert.

Mittagessen wird im allgemeinen von 12.00 bis 14.00 Uhr serviert. Jedes Lokal bietet eine reichhaltige Speisekarte mit Menüs (bestehend aus mindestens 3 Gängen) und Speisen à la carte.

Abendessen wird, falls nicht anders vermerkt, von 18.00 bis 22.00 Uhr serviert. Die Abendspeisekarte unterscheidet sich in ihrer Reichhaltigkeit nur wenig von der Mittagskarte, besonders nicht in größeren Lokalen.

Wichtige Hinweise

Each of these pictures has important information in it. Can you tell your parents (your teacher) what they ought to know?

1.

2.

3.

"Guten Appetit!"

Unsere Küche ist durchgehend offen, von 12 bis 9 Uhr.

4.

Cafe · Restaurant
NICHT NUR FÜR CAMPINGGÄSTE

6.

✗ **Hier** ↰

Rückerstattung der Parkgebühr
beim Verzehr von Speisen

Parkplatz Burg Eltz

Gut bürgerliche Küche

5.

!NEUE ÖFFNUNGSZEITEN!

WARME KÜCHE
VON 11:30 BIS 15:00
17:30 BIS 23:30
SAMSTAGS + SONNTAGS
DURCHGEHEND VON 11:30
BIS 23:30

-MONTAGS RUHETAG-

TÄGLICH PREISWERTE MITTAGSMENÜS MIT SUPPE UND DESSERT

7.

Heute
Ruhetag

8.

Gasthof Kuckuck
BUNDESKEGELBAHN

Binding Bier

Binding Bier

Die Speisekarte

You have gone out for a meal with your parents. As they do not know any German, explain this menu to them (your teacher).

Verwöhnen Sie Ihren Gaumen und fühlen Sie sich wohl

Zur Einstimmung

HERZEN VON MARKTSALATEN MIT SHRIMPSCOCKTAIL — DM 15,50

WACHOLDERGERÄUCHERTES FORELLENFILET
mit Sahnemeerrettich — DM 11,00

EIERSALAT
mit Thunfisch, Zwiebeln und Vinaigrette — DM 8,50

SALATE
frisch aus Nachbar's Garten, mit Schinken und Käsestreifen — DM 6,00

Suppen, die man gerne auslöffelt

SAHNIGE TOMATENSUPPE
mit Gin — DM 6,50

ÜBERBACKENE ZWIEBELSUPPE
mit Käsecroutons und Riesling — DM 5,90

HERZHAFT URIGE LEBERKNÖDELSUPPE
mit Zwiebelschmelze — DM 5,00

Unsere Kleinigkeiten, warm serviert

1/2 DUTZEND SCHNECKEN
in Knoblauchkräuterbutter, Weißbrot — DM 11,50

»BLUTWURSTGERÖSTELTES«
mit Äpfeln und Zwiebeln, Bauernbrot — DM 10,80

KNUSPRIGER KARTOFFELREIBEKUCHEN
mit Schinken und Käse überschmelzt — DM 8,50

GEBACKENER CAMEMBERT
mit gefülltem Preiselbeer-Pfirsich — DM 9,00

»DER KELLERMEISTER-SCHMAUS«
Rühreier mit Speck, auf Vollkornbrot — DM 8,50

Aus unserer Gutsmetzgerei: Deftige Spezialitäten

WÜRZIGER FLEISCHKÄSE
aus der Pfanne, mit Spiegelei und Bauernbrot — DM 7,80

GROBE HAUSMACHER BRATWÜRSTE -1 Paar-
so richtig nach »Pfälzer Art«, mit Weinsauerkraut — DM 8,50

KNACKIGE DEIDESHEIMER WÜRSTCHEN
mit Meerrettich — DM 7,00

WEINKRÜGERS ROASTBRATWÜRSTLE
würzig knusprig gebraten — DM 7,80

Aus dem Schmorkessel

RIESLING-RAHM-GULASCH
vom Kalb, mit Spätzle — DM 14,00

LECKERER SAUERBRATEN
hausgemacht, mit Rosinen, geschmelzte Kartoffelknödel — DM 16,50

BÄUERLICHE RINDSROULADE
mit Zwiebeln und Speck gefüllt, Rotweinsauce, Erbsen und Kartoffelpüree — DM 15,50

Diese Karte ist das erste Motiv pfälzischer Kunst, geschaffen von Klaus Schaurer. Jährlich wird ein weiteres Motiv folgen und dem Sammler die Möglichkeit geben, eine eigene, reizvolle Galerie anzulegen.
Klaus Rainer Schaurer, 1939 in Kaiserslautern geboren, seit 1968 Mitglied der Arbeitsgemeinschaft Pälzer Künstler. Künstlerische Arbeiten an öffentlichen Gebäuden, zahlreiche Einzel- und Gemeinschaftsausstellungen im In- und Ausland.
Edition: Druckerei und Verlag Hans H. Englram, 6733 Haßloch/Pfalz

Sorgfältig gebrutzelt

WEINKRÜGERS STEAK-TOAST
mit Champignons und Camembert überbacken, Räucherschinkenscheibe   DM 16,00

DER STECK'L WICK'L ... seit eh' und je begehrt
mit gebratenem Kartoffelküchle und Salat vom Markt   DM 16,00

SAFTIGES KELTERHAUSSTEAK
vom Schweinenacken, mit glacierten Zwiebeln und Bratkartoffeln   DM 17,00

RÜCKENNÜSSCHEN
vom Jungschwein, Kräuterbutter, erfrischender Salatteller   DM 18,00

ZARTES LENDCHEN DER EIDGENOSSEN
mit Emmentaler überschmelzt, Schinkensahne, Kartoffelreibekuchen   DM 19,00

OCHSENSTEAK
mit gestoßenem Pfeffer, Kräuterbutter, Bratkartoffeln   DM 21,00

Aus der Käseschachtel

BUNTE KÄSEWÜRFEL
mit Früchten und Brezeln garniert   DM 8,50

HOBELSPÄNE
... von Original Greyerzer   DM 8,00

DAS KÄSE-RACELETTE NACH WALLISER ART
mit Perlzwiebeln, gebratenem Speck und Kartoffeln   DM 13,80

REICHHALTIGE KÄSEAUSWAHL
.... auf einem Teller   DM 14,50

Die Vesper-Ecke mit Hausmacher Spezialitäten

SCHINKEN AUS DEM REBHOLZRAUCH
auf Bauernbrot   DM 9,50

WURSTSALAT
deftig angemacht, mit Gürkchen und Zwiebeln   DM 7,80

LÄNDLICHE WINZER-SCHNITTE
mit Original Pfälzer Leber- und Griebenwurst   DM 7,50

WEINKRÜGERS SCHLEMMER-SALAT-SCHÜSSEL
mit Artischockenherzen, Thunfisch, Tomaten, Ei,
Wurstsalat, Gartensalat und Zwiebelringen   DM 13,00

DAS GROSSE GUTSHOF-VESPER
mit Schinken, Schwartenmagen, Räucherwurst, original Sauschwänzel
und einem Glas hausgebranntem Trester   DM 15,80

Für Schleckermäulchen

APFELKÜCHLE
mit Vanillesoße   DM 4,50

DER SÜSSE PFANNKUCHEN
gefüllt mit Blaubeeren, Vanilleeis und Kirschwässerle   DM 8,00

EISSPIEGELEIER
mit Aprikosen und Sahne   DM 5,50

Beachten Sie auch unsere aktuellen Tagesangebote.
Eisspezialitäten finden Sie auf unserer Eiskarte, fragen Sie Ihre Serviererin.
Mehrwertsteuer und Service sind in unseren Preisen enthalten.
Konservierungsstoffe: 1-Benzoesäure, 2-Sorbinsäure, 3-Farbstoff, 4-Geschwefelt, 5-Geschwärzt

Hör zu! ❺

You will hear a conversation which takes place in a restaurant. While you listen to the recording the first time, make notes about the following:

a) What drinks do Harald, Susi, Gabi and Rolf order?
b) What does each person order to eat?
c) Who pays the bill?

Jetzt bist du dran!

A Listen to the first part of the recording again, and note down how Harald asks for a table for four. Working with a partner, practise this short dialogue. Ask for a table for one, two, three, four, five and six people. Change roles each time.

B Now listen to the section where people order their drinks again. Work in groups of four or five and act out a similar situation. Change roles so that each of you takes the role of the waiter/waitress as well.

C Make sure that you have all got a copy of worksheet A. Listen to the next section of the recording again. Working in groups of four or five, order your meal. Change roles so that more than one of you plays the waiter.

D Listen to the last section of the recording again and note how Harald asks for the bill and how the waiter asks whether they have enjoyed their meal and how they would like to pay. Then act out a similar situation, working in pairs. One of you assumes the role of waiter, the other that of the customer.

E Work in pairs, with one of you assuming the role of the customer and the other that of the waiter/waitress.

Customer:

Go into a restaurant – attract the waiter's attention – ask for the menu – order something to drink – when you have made up your mind, order your meal – starter? main course? sweet? – ask for the bill.

Waiter:

Greet the customer – offer him/her a menu. Perhaps he/she would like something to drink – ask him/her if he/she is ready to order – ask him/her if he/she would like a starter – collect his/her plate – ask him/her if he/she enjoyed the meal – perhaps he/she would like a dessert – bid the customer a polite farewell.

Use either the menu reproduced on pages 114 and 115 or the one on your worksheet (worksheet A of this unit) to help you choose your meal. The box contains some phrases you may want to use:

Bitte schön	Vorspeise
Darf ich bitte . . .	Hauptgericht
die Speisekarte	Nachspeise/Nachtisch
Ich hätte gern . . .	Hat es Ihnen geschmeckt?
Ich möchte gern . . .	Stimmt so
Möchten Sie schon bestellen?	ein Trinkgeld
Herr Ober!	Fräulein!
	Bedienung!

Hör zu! ❻

Sometimes service in a restaurant is not quite what it should be. Listen to what the following people have to say to the waiter/waitress and match each phrase with the appropriate picture below.

Jetzt bist du dran!

Working in pairs, act out similar situations, complaining about one of the things in the illustrations, or making up your own complaints.

E. Das Essen zu Hause

Schweizer Mahlzeiten

Read what Karin Elsener has to say about what people in Switzerland eat and at what time of day.

Karin

„Bei uns Schweizern gibt es drei Hauptmahlzeiten: das Frühstück, das Mittagessen und das Abendessen. Als Zwischenmahlzeiten kennen wir den „Z'nüni" und den „Z'vieri", die um 9 Uhr morgens, bzw. um 16 Uhr nachmittags eingenommen werden. Der „Z'vieri" ist jedoch vor allem für die Kinder gedacht.

Zum Frühstück essen wir meistens Butterbrot mit Marmelade und trinken Tee, Kaffee, Fruchtsaft oder heiße Schokolade dazu. Viele essen auch Joghurt mit Haferflocken und frischen Früchten.

Der „Z'nüni" wird in der großen Pause eingenommen. Er besteht aus einem Apfel, einem Butterbrot oder aus Gebäck oder Schokolade.

Das Mittagessen besteht aus einer warmen Speise und einem Salat, z.B. Fleisch, Teigwaren oder Kartoffeln, Gemüse oder Salat.

Der „Z'vieri" wird um vier Uhr nachmittags gegessen und besteht aus Tee und Obst oder süßem Gebäck.

Das Abendessen gleicht dem Frühstück, wird aber noch durch Käse, Aufschnitt oder aufgewärmte Reste vom Mittagessen ergänzt. Es wird so gegen 18 Uhr eingenommen."

(Karin Elsener 15, Rheineck)

Jetzt schreibst du!

Write a letter to your penfriend telling him/her about mealtimes in your home. Say what kind of things you eat and when.

Tischgespräche

The grid below contains the kind of questions you may be asked or wish to ask at table, as well as phrases expressing how to respond to questions about whether you wish second helpings at mealtimes. Read it carefully.

Questions			Answers
Möchtest du noch	einen Apfelsaft eine Cola eine Limo ein Glas Bier ein Glas Wein eine Tasse Kaffee eine Tasse Tee		Nein, danke. Danke, nein. Ja gern. Nein, ich kann nicht mehr. Nein danke, das reicht. Nein, ich bin satt. Ja danke. Danke, ein bißchen. Danke, ein wenig. Ja bitte. Es schmeckt ausgezeichnet. Danke. Aber nur ein paar (Würstchen, Kartoffeln, etc.).
	eine Scheibe Brot ein Stück Kuchen ein Stück Fleisch eine Tomate		
(Möchtest du) noch etwas?	Salat Gurkensalat Blumenkohl Käse Wurst		
Darf ich noch	Soße Sahne Kompott Butter } haben		Aber natürlich. Bitte. Sicher. Gern. Selbstverständlich. Gern. Bedien dich.
Noch ein paar	Karotten Erbsen Kartoffeln } bitte		

Jetzt bist du dran!

Working in pairs, use the grid to form conversations with your partner in which one of you offers the other some more food or drink or asks for more of something, and the other responds accordingly.

IM BERUF

 UNIT

1 3

In this unit you will practise:
- ▷ talking about your job,
- ▶ expressing job and career aspirations,
- ▷ talking about what you expect your future job to offer,
- ▶ reading newspaper advertisements for jobs.

A. Berufswünsche

Was sind sie von Beruf?

A Look at these pictures and tell your teacher the German name of the job each person has.

B Now read the two sets of captions below. Match each picture with the right caption to say who does what and where.

1. Sortiert Briefe und trägt sie aus.
2. Hilft kranken Leuten.
3. Backt Brot und Brötchen.
4. Fliegt Touristen in andere Länder.
5. Zerlegt und verkauft Fleisch und Wurst.
6. Kocht Speisen.
7. Unterrichtet Kinder.

a) Praxis/Krankenhaus.
b) Bäckerei.
c) Schule.
d) Metzgerei.
e) Post.
f) Flugzeug.
g) Küche.

Hör zu! ❶

Some people are going to tell you what their job is. Listen carefully and write down in each case:

a) the name of the job,
b) any other relevant fact about the person's job.

Hör zu! ❷

Listen to these four young people talking about what they would like to become when they leave school. Note down for each person what job they would like to do, and why.

Jetzt bist du dran!

Using similar questions to the ones you have just heard, ask your classmates what they would like to do when they leave school.

Meine Zukunftspläne

Here are three other German pupils writing about their plans for the future. Read the passages. Then tell your teacher about the job each one of them hopes to do in the future.

Ina:

„Im Moment gehe ich in die elfte Klasse eines Gymnasiums. Wenn ich mein Abitur geschafft habe, werde ich wahrscheinlich studieren, und zwar Außenarchitektur. Ich möchte gerne Architektin werden, weil ich gerne zeichne und mit Menschen zusammen sein will. Außerdem will ich später auch ein Haus haben. Im Moment muß ich allerdings erst einmal pauken. Bis zum Abitur habe ich ja noch genug Zeit."

Ina

Mona

Mona:

„Ich gehe noch zur Realschule. Wenn ich mit der Schule fertig bin, möchte ich Automechanikerin werden. Ich habe mich schon immer für Technik interessiert und helfe meinem Vater immer dabei, sein Auto zu reparieren. Ich hoffe, daß ich einen Ausbildungsplatz in einer Werkstatt finden kann."

Achim

Achim:

„Ich interessiere mich für das Theater und für Kunst überhaupt. Darum möchte ich einmal als Maskenbildner arbeiten. Die Ausbildung ist ziemlich hart und dauert drei Jahre. Aber man lernt unheimlich viel. Ein Maskenbildner macht alles, die Masken, das Make-up und die Frisuren für die Schauspieler. Ich helfe jetzt schon manchmal im örtlichen Theater aus."

Hör zu! ❸

A number of people have been asked if they are happy with their job. Note down for each speaker whether they are satisfied or not, and the reason given.

Zeitungsinserate

Read the advertisements below. The following people are looking for employment. Can you tell them which advertisement they might reply to?

a) A friend of yours, who wishes to work as an au pair.

b) Your German cousin, who loves flowers.

Au-Pair Mädchen
junge Familie m. einjähr. Felix sucht Mädchen bis 21 J. für Kinderbetreuung und leichte Haushaltsarbeiten für 1 Jahr. Eigenes Zi. mit Du/WC. TV wird gestellt. Bewerbung bitte schriftlich mit Lichtbild (zurück) und Tel.-Nr. an Familie Duczek, Wogenmannsburg 10, 2 Hamburg 61

KFZ-Betrieb mit Mietfahrzeugen sucht weiblichen
Bürokaufmann
für Frühschicht im Alter zwischen 20 und 40 Jahren bei guter Bezahlung zum baldigen Eintritt.
☎ 2016900, Frau Ringmeier.

Das Neurolog. Krankenhaus München sucht z. 1. Okt. 85 od. später eine (n)
Koch/Köchin
Diätische Schulung bzw. entsprechende Kenntnisse wären wünschenswert. Wir sind eine Fachklinik mit 108 Betten. Tägl. werden ca. 150 Essen-Vollportionen hergestellt. Wir bieten Vergütung nach **BAT** mit allen Sozialleistungen des öffentl. Dienstes. Bewerbung erbeten an die Verwaltung des **Neurol. Krankenhauses**, Tristanstr. 20,8000 München 40, ☎ 089/364056

Suche ab 1.10. junge, freundliche
Floristin
die selbständig und kreativ arbeiten möchte. ☎ 08123/562

Maler
bei übertariflicher Bezahlung für sofort gesucht. ☎ 325814

B. Wie es wirklich ist

Frauen über ihren Beruf

Read the three passages below and on the following page, in which women talk about their jobs. In each case note down in your notebook:

a) what the job is,
b) what has to be done,
c) the daily routine,
d) what the person likes/dislikes.

Özyni:

„Ich heiße Özyni und bin seit drei Jahren als Fabrikarbeiterin bei der Firma Klefisch tätig. Ich habe bei Klefisch angefangen, als ich aus der Türkei nach Deutschland als Gastarbeiterin kam. Hier werden allerlei Sachen aus Stahl hergestellt. Ich arbeite in der Gießerei. Die Arbeit ist sehr schwer, hauptsächlich, weil es immer sehr heiß ist. Ich fange morgens um 6 Uhr an und habe um 4 Uhr nachmittags Feierabend. Am Samstag mache ich von 6 bis 11 Uhr Überstunden. Sonntags habe ich frei. Ich muß dabei helfen, die schweren Stahlsachen zum Einpacken fertigzumachen. In der Gießerei gibt es immer viel Lärm, und sehr schmutzig ist es auch. Ich freue mich immer, wenn Feierabend ist."

Özyni (zweite von links)

Astrid:

„Ich heiße Astrid und bin seit vier Jahren Sekretärin beim ZDF. Ich fange morgens um 8 Uhr an. Um 12 haben wir eine Stunde Mittagspause, und dann machen wir bis 16.30 Uhr weiter. Mein Arbeitstag fängt mit einer Besprechung im Büro meiner Chefin an. Sie erklärt uns, was im Laufe des Tages gemacht werden muß. Ich muß meistens Briefe an verschiedene Firmen tippen, die unsere Kunden sind. Am liebsten stenographiere ich. Meine Arbeit macht mir Spaß. Ich verstehe mich gut mit meiner Chefin, ich verdiene gut und habe fünf Wochen Urlaub im Jahr. Ich bin sehr zufrieden."

Astrid

Helga:

„Ich heiße Helga Braun, bin 44 Jahre alt und arbeite als Krankenpflegerin in einem Pflegeheim für behinderte Kinder. Die Arbeit mit behinderten Jugendlichen ist schwer. Sie erfordert Geschicklichkeit und Geduld, ein offenes Ohr zu jeder Zeit und eine große Portion Stehvermögen. Ich mache diese Arbeit seit 14 Jahren. Sie gibt mir sehr viel Kraft und füllt mich vollends aus. Ich arbeite meistens nachts. Wenn es draußen hell wird, habe ich Feierabend. Dann wartet der Haushalt."

Helga

C. Arbeitslosigkeit

And now the problem of unemployment. Read the passage below, which is a newspaper extract, and answer the question which follows.

Im Winter 150 000 neue Arbeitslose

Hamburg (dpa) – Im Monat Dezember nimmt die Arbeitslosenzahl normalerweise ab. Dieses Jahr sieht es jedoch anders aus. Es wird damit gerechnet, daß rund 150 000 Menschen neu arbeitslos sein werden. Die Gesamtzahl wird etwa 2,34 Millionen sein. Falls es nicht zu einem starken Wintereinbruch kommen sollte, könnten die Werte etwas darunter bleiben.

(Ruhr Nachrichten)

Kapiert?

What is the significance of the figures 150 000 and 2.34 million?

SPORT [UNIT] 14

In this unit you will practise:

▷ talking about your sports interests,
▶ asking about sports facilities,
▷ buying tickets for sports events.

A. Was kann man spielen?

Was für Sport treibst du gern?

Look at these pictograms depicting various types of sports. Tell your teacher which sports you are interested in and actively pursue.

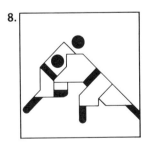

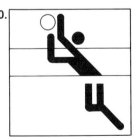

Hör zu! ❶

Listen to these people talking about the sports they pursue. Write down in your notebook what each person does.

Meine Hobbys

You have found the following article in a German youth magazine. Read it carefully.

Hallo . . .

Ich heiße Andrea und bin 16 Jahre alt.

Meine interessantesten Hobbys sind Fußball und Wasserski fahren. Zusammen mit mir haben sich noch mehrere Mädchen aus meiner Klasse und aus der näheren Umgebung dazu entschlossen, eine Fußballmannschaft zu gründen.

Unser erstes Spiel haben wir zwar nicht gewonnen, aber gefeiert haben wir danach trotzdem. Ich finde, daß ein Hobby dazu da ist, Spaß und Unterhaltung zu bringen und eine Freizeitbeschäftigung zu sein. Wir hatten insgesamt schon vier Fußballspiele, aber da jetzt der Winter kommt, geht unsere „Fußballsaison" erst nächstes Frühjahr weiter.

Wie gesagt, fahre ich auch Wasserski. Das macht mir unheimlich viel Spaß. Zuerst fand ich es unheimlich schwierig. Ich bin ständig ins Wasser gefallen, und das gar nicht immer sanft. Aber so nach und nach habe ich es gelernt.

7

Kapiert?

Your parents are interested in the article. Tell them about Andrea's sports interests.

Jetzt bist du dran!

A You wish to find out more about your German exchange partner's interests. Ask him/her the following questions:

1. Was spielst du?
2. Wo spielst du . . . ?
3. Seit wann spielst du . . . ?
4. Wie oft in der Woche spielst du . . . . ?

5. Bist du Mitglied in einem Verein?
6. Spielst du für eine Mannschaft?
7. Ist es teuer, . . . zu spielen?
8. Wie gut kannst du . . . spielen?

B Act out the following two roleplays with your partner.

1. You: Ask if he/she likes sport.
   Your partner: Say you do and name the three sports you play.
   You: Ask how often he/she goes training.
   Your partner: Say you go training three times a week.
   You: Ask if he/she is a member of a club.
   Your partner: Say which club you belong to. Say you play for the junior team.
   You: Choose one of the sports he/she mentioned earlier and ask if he/she likes to watch it on TV.
   Your partner: Say you prefer to play it – it's much more fun.

   Here are some useful expressions to help you with your conversation:
   das Training – wie oft? – einmal/zweimal/dreimal in der Woche/die Woche – Mitglied eines Vereins/ich bin im . . . –verein – die Jugendmannschaft – das macht Spaß!

2. You: Ask if he/she likes sports.
   Your partner: Say you do and name your favourite sport. Say you used to play another sport as well, but now you have too much work to do for school.
   You: Ask how long he/she has been playing his/her favourite sport.
   Your partner: Tell him/her how long.
   You: Ask him/her if he/she plays every Saturday.
   Your partner: Say yes and add another evening as well.
   You: Ask whether or not he/she plays this sport at school.
   Your partner: Say yes, on Monday afternoons and on Wednesdays in your lunch-break.

Jetzt schreibst du!

Your exchange partner is the editor of a school magazine. He/she has asked you to write a short article about the sports you are involved in. Following Andrea's example, write such an article.

Möchtest du das auch machen? 📖

Look at these photographs of different types of sports and famous German sports personalities. Match each photograph with one of the captions below:

a) Die beiden erfolgreichsten deutschen Bobfahrer: Wolfgang Zimmerer und Manfred Schumann. Bei den Olympischen Spielen errangen sie die Silbermedaille im Zweierbob.

b) Der Skilanglauf findet in der Bundesrepublik immer mehr Anhänger.

c) Fechten wird in der Bundesrepublik nicht nur als Leistungssport betrieben, sondern auch als Freizeitbeschäftigung.

d) Gerd Wiltfang, erfolgreicher deutscher Springreiter.

e) Toni Mang, Motorradweltmeister in den Klassen 250 und 350 ccm.

f) Dieter Thurau, Favorit zahlreicher Radrennen.

1.

2.

3.

4.

5.

6.

B. Wo kann man spielen?

Wo spielt man das?

Look at the pictures. Can you tell your teacher what is depicted in each one?
Tell him/her the German name of the sport.

Wo ist Sport-Billy?

Read the captions below. Match each caption with the correct picture.

a) auf der Skipiste
b) auf dem Fußballplatz
c) auf dem Tennisplatz
d) in der Turnhalle
e) im Stadion
f) auf der Laufbahn

g) auf der Eisbahn
h) auf dem See
i) im Boxring
j) auf der Radrennbahn
k) im Schwimmbad

Jetzt bist du dran!

A You are working in the tourist information office in Hamburg. A tourist (your teacher will take this part) is coming in and asks you the following questions. Can you answer him/her using the information supplied?

1. Bei diesem schönen Wetter möchte ich schwimmen gehen. Gibt es hier in der Nähe ein Freibad?
2. Meine Frau und ich sind in einem Kegelverein. Haben Sie die Telefonnummer von einem Hotel oder einem Gasthaus mit einer Bundeskegelbahn?
3. Kann man hier auch im Dezember noch Minigolf spielen?
4. Gibt es in der Nähe eine Sauna?
5. Gibt es einen Segelclub? Wie heißt er?

B Carry out a roleplay with your partner. One of you is the tourist, the other the person in the tourist information office.

Here is some vocabulary to help you:

Ich . . . gern.
Wieviel kostet das?
Wo ist in der Nähe . . . ?
Wie ist die Telefonnummer?
Wo kann ich hier . . . ?

Gibt es hier in der Gegend . . . ?
Wie sind die Öffnungszeiten?
Bis um wieviel Uhr kann man . . . ?

Minigolf (Stadtpark)
Ganzjährig geöffnet
Entritt: DM 6,–
Tel.: 62 01 84.

Segeln
Norddeutscher Regattaverein an der Alster. Weitere Informationen erhältlich von: Hamburg 97 24 10.

Kegeln
Bundeskegelbahnen finden Sie in den folgenden Hotels:
Atlantic Hotel, tel.: 24 80 01
Reichshof, tel.: 24 83 30
Landhaus zum Lindenkrug, tel.: 60 48 00.

Schwimmen
Holthusenfreibad (Goernestraße)
Öffnungszeiten: 07.30 bis 21.00 (während der Freibadsaison)
Eintritt: Kinder DM 2,50
　　　　　Erwachsene DM 5,–
Sauna DM 12,–.
Hallenbad
Öffnungszeiten: 07.30 bis 21.00.
Eintritt: Kinder DM 2,–
　　　　　Erwachsene DM 4,–.

Hör zu! ❷

Listen to these people, who are wanting to watch or take part in some sporting activity. For each conversation, note down the following:

a) the activity,
b) tickets or similar purchased,
c) cost of tickets,
d) any equipment hired, and cost,
e) any other relevant information, instructions or conditions.

Jetzt bist du dran!

Carry out these roleplays with your partner.

1. You want to buy a ticket to see a football match.

    You: Tell the assistant you would like a ticket for the football match on Wednesday night.

    Assistant: Welches Spiel?

    You: Tell him you want to see the cup match between 1. FC Köln and Leverkusen.

    Assistant: Was für eine Karte möchtest du?

    You: Tell him you would like a ticket for the north end of the stadium.

    Assistant: Eingang 21. Geht das?

    You: Tell him that's fine and ask him how much it costs.

    Assistant: DM 6,50.

    You: Hand him the money and thank him.

    Here are some useful words:

    ein Pokalspiel – Schülerkarte – Nordkurve

2. You want to book a tennis court.

    You: Tell the lady in charge you would like a court for the afternoon.

    Assistant: Um wieviel Uhr?

    You: Tell her the time you would like it.

    Assistant: Laß mich mal gucken. Nein, zu der Zeit sind alle Plätze besetzt.

    You: Give her an alternative.

    Assistant: Ist in Ordnung.

    You: Ask her how much it costs per hour.

    Assistant: DM 12.

    You: Say you don't have any rackets or balls. Ask if you could hire those, too.

    Assistant: Ja, natürlich. Der Schläger kostet DM 3,50 und drei Bälle DM 2.

    You: Tell her how many rackets and balls you need.

    Assistant: Schläger und Bälle haben wir genug. Bis heute nachmittag.

Hör zu! ❸

Stefan and Silke are discussing what they should do.

a) What is suggested?

b) Why do they decide not to do a particular thing?

c) What do they do in the end?

Jetzt bist du dran!

Discuss with your partner what you should do this Saturday morning. To help you, there is a list below of possible things to do and a list of reasons for doing them, or excuses for not doing them.

Suggestion:	Negative response:	Positive response:

ins Schwimmbad gehen
Volleyball spielen
zur Turnhalle gehen
mit dem Rad fahren
Fußball spielen
einen Dauerlauf machen
Tennis spielen
Krafttraining machen
Schlittschuhlaufen
Squash spielen
	macht keinen Spaß
	anstrengend
	langweilig
	zu viele Leute
	müde
	muß Hausaufgaben machen
	muß in die Stadt gehen
	möchte Schallplatten kaufen
	es regnet
	es ist zu kalt/heiß
	kein Geld
		macht Spaß
		kostet nichts
		es ist schön warm
		der Platz ist hier in der Nähe
		heute gibt es keinen Wind
		ich habe gerade neue Schuhe
		  gekauft
		ich möchte meinen neuen Schläger
		  ausprobieren

Ein Brief von Karin

Opposite is a letter you have just received from your penpal, telling you about the International Athletics Match she has just been to.

Jetzt schreibst du!

Write back, describing a sports event which you have been to recently:

a) What was it?
b) Where?
c) Who did you go with?
d) Was anyone famous participating?
e) Who played well/badly?
f) What was the score?
g) What did the papers say?

Aachen, den 8. August

Liebe Sharon,

Vielen Dank für Deine Ansichtskarte aus Brighton.
Es freut mich, daß es Dir und Deiner Familie dort
so gut gefallen hat.
Ich war am Wochenende mit Uschi beim Internationalen
Leichtathletikfest in Köln. Im Müngersdorfer Stadion
waren 50 000 Zuschauer. Die Stimmung war wirklich
einmalig. Der 400-Meter-Lauf hat mir am besten
gefallen. Die Weltmeisterin aus der DDR hat gewonnen
und dabei einen neuen Weltrekord aufgestellt.
Den 1500-Meter-Lauf hat Brigitte Kraus vom
ASV Köln gewonnen. Das war wirklich toll. Wir
haben alle geklatscht und gejubelt. Nächstes Jahr
gehen wir wieder dahin. Es hat wirklich Spaß gemacht.

So Sharon, ich muß jetzt leider Schluß machen.
Meine Mutter hat mich gerade zum Essen gerufen.

Viele liebe Grüße auch an Deine Familie.

Alles Liebe

Karin

VERKEHRSMITTEL

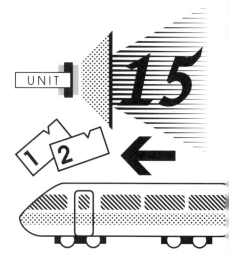

In this unit you will practise:

▶ asking for information on public transport,
▷ understanding announcements,
▶ buying the correct ticket,
▷ asking directions.

A. Die Bahn

Hör zu! ❶

A While you are waiting at a railway station in Germany, you overhear these conversations. Which facilities do the people want to use?

B Look at the photographs below. Match each conversation with the correct photograph.

a

b

c

d

Hör zu! ❷

Listen to the following announcements at various platforms of a railway station in Germany.

A For announcements 1–3, note down:
   a) the platform number,
   b) where the train is from,
   c) where it is going to,
   d) the departure time.

B For announcements 4–6, note down:
   a) the arrival platform,
   b) the connections,
   c) the departure time.

Hör zu! ❸

Listen to the following two conversations. Copy the grid opposite into your notebook and complete it.

	1	2
Pieces of luggage		
Type of luggage		
Kept for how long		
Fee		
Any other information		

Jetzt bist du dran!

Work in pairs. One of you takes the role of the clerk at the left luggage office, the other that of the customer. Change roles once you have been through each situation.

1. **You:** Say hello and ask if you could leave your rucksack till tonight.
   Clerk: Ja, natürlich. Wann wollen Sie das Gepäck wieder abholen?
   You: Say about 7 pm.
   Clerk: Das tut mir leid, wir schließen um 18.30 Uhr.
   You: Say that's OK, you will come before 6.30 pm. Ask how much it is.
   Clerk: Das macht 1,50 DM, bitte.
   You: Hand over the money and ask for a receipt.
   Clerk: Hier, dieser Nummernschein ist Ihre Quittung. Den müssen Sie wieder mitbringen, wenn Sie das Gepäck abholen.
   You: Thank him/her and say goodbye.

2. **Clerk:** Guten Tag!
   You: Say hello and say that you would like to leave your case here until tomorrow afternoon. Ask how much it costs.
   Clerk: Das wäre dann DM 2,30. Um wieviel Uhr holen Sie Ihren Koffer wieder ab?
   You: Say that your train leaves at 3.45, so you will collect your case at about 3.30.
   Clerk: Ist in Ordnung. So, Ihr Schein. Den müssen Sie mitbringen, wenn Sie Ihren Koffer abholen.
   You: Thank him/her.

Urlaub mit dem Fahrrad, mit der Bahn 📖

You are planning to go on a cycling holiday with a few friends. The tourist office has given you this leaflet. Read it carefully.

Tell your friends if:

a) you can take your bike on the train,

b) when you have to check your bike in,

c) what you do if you wish to hire a bike instead of taking your own.

Sie kommen zügig a Ihr Fahrrad auch.

Wenn Sie mit der Bahn auf Urlaubsreise gehen, brauchen Sie selbstverständlich nicht auf Ihr Fahrrad zu verzichten. Die Bahn fährt es im Gepäckwagen bis an Ihr Urlaubsziel. Zu den Hauptreisezeiten im Sommer sollten Sie Ihr Rad jedoch möglichst 3 Tage vor der Abreise aufgeben. So ist sichergestellt, daß Sie es bei der Gepäckabfertigung Ihres Zielbahnhofs abholen können, wenn Sie dort ankommen. Übrigens können Sie auch an vielen Bahnhöfen ein Fahrrad mieten, wenn Sie möchten. Über das „Wo" und „Wie" informiert Sie eine spezielle Broschüre, die Sie an jeder Gepäck-abfertigung bekommen.

Hör zu! ❹ 📼

Listen to the conversations of people asking about train times. Copy the grid below into your notebook and complete it.

Customer:	1	2	3	etc.
Departure: Arrival: Place: Platform: Time: Other information: Name/No. of train:				

Jetzt bist du dran! 💬

A Work in pairs. Using the timetable opposite, imagine you are an official at the information desk. It is nearly 11 a.m. on a Thursday. Various tourists (your partner takes their roles) approach you with their enquiries. Answer their questions.

Tourist A asks:

1. Wann fährt der nächste Zug nach Hamm, bitte?
2. Was ist das für ein Zug?

Tourist B asks:

1. Mit welchem Zug komme ich am schnellsten nach München?
2. Muß ich da Zuschlag bezahlen?

Tourist C asks:

1. Von welchem Bahnsteig fährt der nächste Zug nach Hamburg?

Tourist D asks:

1. Wann fährt der „Hellas"–Express ab und von welchem Bahnsteig?
2. Wann komme ich in Belgrad an?
3. Kann ich ein Bett im Schlafwagen reservieren?

B Now you want to make some enquiries. It is 8.05 pm on a Saturday and you ask the official (your partner):

a) when the next train leaves for Hamburg,

b) from which platform it leaves,

c) whether you can get something to eat on board,

d) what time it gets in.

Zeichenerklärung

Am 6. VI. Verkehr wie †

Die Züge führen im allgemeinen die 1. und 2. Wagenklasse
Abweichungen sind unter der Zugnummer besonders angegeben.

IC	= Intercity-Zug. (IC-Zuschlag erforderlich. Entgelt für Platzreservierung im IC-Zuschlag enthalten, für Reisegruppen Platzreservierung erforderlich.) Verbundfahrausweise gelten nicht.
FD	= Fern-Express, qualifizierter Schnellzug Verbundfahrausweise gelten nicht.
D	= Schnellzug
M	= Messeschnellzug; nur 1. Klasse Verbundfahrausweise gelten nicht.
E ohne Buchstaben	= Eilzug
	= Zug des Nahverkehrs
1	= Zu Fahrausweisen bis 50 km sowie zu Streckenzeitkarten ist Schnellzugzuschlag erforderlich Verbundfahrausweise gelten nicht
	= Durchlaufende Wagen (Kurswagen)
	= Schlafwagen
	= Liegewagen 2. Klasse
	= Zugrestaurant
	= Quick-Pick-Zugrestaurant
	= Speisen und Getränke im Zug erhältlich
	= verkehrt nicht täglich oder nur während eines bestimmten Zeitabschnittes

11.00

11.02	E 3263	Kamen 11.14 – Hamm 11.24 – Gütersloh 12.12 – Bielefeld 12.26 – Herford 12.37 – Bad Salzuflen 12.52 – Detmold 13.13 – **Horn-Bad Meinberg 13.29** (-Altenbeken)	10 a/b
✗ 11.02	3453 ⑥	DO Westfalenhalle 11.07 – DO-Hörde 11.11 – Holzwickede 11.22 – Unna 11.27 – **Hamm 11.50**	4
11.10	3656 3666	Gelsenkirchen 11.35 – Oberhausen 11.54 – **Duisburg 12.01**	21 a/b
11.11	D 453	Hamm 11.28 – Soest 11.56 – Paderborn 12.39 – Altenbeken 12.54 – Warburg 13.25 – Kassel 14.05 – Bebra 14.55 – Eisenach 16.59 – Erfurt 18.00 – Weimar 18.26 – Naumburg 18.55 – **Leipzig 19.50**	11 a/b
11.18	IC 518	*Schwabenpfeil* Hamm 11.33 – Bielefeld 12.00 – **Hannover 12.49**	10 a/b
11.20	D 411	*Hellas-Express* Gelsenkirchen 11.46 – Oberhausen 12.05 – Düsseldorf 12.38 – Neuss 12.55 – Köln 13.23 – Bonn-Beuel 13.53 – Koblenz 14.34 – Mainz 15.32 – Mannheim 16.31 – Stuttgart 18.16 – Ulm 19.37 – Augsburg 20.31 – München 21.19 – Salzburg 23.22 – Jesenice 3.30 – Ljubljana 5.10 – Zagreb 8.08 – Belgrad 14.00 – Skopje 22.02 – Gevgelija 0.42 – Thessaloniki 4.30 (MZ) – **Athen 14.40** (MZ) (3. Tag) *Platzkartenpflichtig für Reisende nach dem Ausland*	18 a/b
11.22	5327	DO-Barop 11.28 – **Witten 11.38**	5
11.27	IC 639	*Germania* Münster 11.55 – Osnabrück 12.19 – Bremen 13.11 – Hamburg Hbf 14.06 – HH Dammtor 14.12 – **Hamburg-Altona 14.20**	10 a/b
11.29	6168 2.	DO Westfalenhalle 11.34 – DO Tierpark 11.37 – Herdecke 11.51 – Hagen 12.01 – ✗ Brügge 12.46 – ✗ **Lüdenscheid 12.57**	2
11.31	5235	Kamen 11.47 – **Hamm 11.59**	7
11.35	IC 509	*Kommodore* Bochum 11.47 – Essen 11.58 – Duisburg 12.11 – Düsseldorf 12.26 – Köln 12.50 – Bonn 13.11 – Koblenz 13.45 – Wiesbaden 14.41 – **Frankfurt 15.11**	16 a/b
11.35	7619 7019	DO-Derne 11.43 – Lünen 11.50 – ✗ Lüdinghausen 12.11 – ✗ Dülmen 12.20 – ✗ Coesfeld 12.44 – ✗ außer ⑥ Ahaus 13.10 – **Gronau 13.33** *Hält nicht in DO Hoesch*	23 a/b
11.43	E 3491 ③)	DO Westfalenhalle 11.49 – DO-Hörde 11.54 – DO-Aplerbeck Süd 11.58 – Schwerte 12.05 – Fröndenberg 12.23 – Arnsberg 12.47 – Bestwig 13.16 – **Brilon Wald 13.33** – ✗ außer ⑥ **Messinghausen 13.44**	✗ 3 † 7
11.44	IC 523	*Heinrich der Löwe* Essen 12.04 – Duisburg 12.17 – Düsseldorf 12.32 – Köln 12.56 – Bonn 13.18 – Koblenz 13.51 – Mainz 14.41 – F Flughafen ✈ 14.58 – Frankfurt 15.13 – Würzburg 16.34 – Augsburg 18.30 – **München 19.03** *Hält nicht in Bochum*	11 a/b
✗ 11.47	5722	Castrop-Rauxel Süd 12.14 – Herne 12.23 – **Wanne-Eickel 12.31**	18 a/b
11.49	IC 613	*Kurpfalz* Hagen 12.10 – W-Elberfeld 12.26 – Köln 12.56 – Bonn 13.22 – Koblenz 13.57 – Mainz 14.47 – Mannheim 15.27 – Heidelberg 15.42 – Stuttgart 16.51 – Ulm 17.52 – Augsburg 18.35 – **München 19.08**	16 a/b

20.00

20.09	E 3015	Kamen 20.17 – **Hamm 20.26**	20 a/b
✗ 20.12 außer ⑥	5177	DO-Derne 20.22 – **Lünen 20.28**	23 a/b
20.18	IC 106	*Lötschberg* Hamm 20.33 – Bielefeld 21.00 – **Hannover 21.49**	10 a/b
20.22	5365	DO-Barop 20.28 – **Witten 20.38**	✗ 5 † 4
† 20.23	5281	Kamen 20.38 – **Hamm 20.50**	7
20.27 außer ⑥, nicht 16. VI.	IC 504	*Senator* Münster 20.55 – Osnabrück 21.19 – Bremen 22.11 – HH-Harburg 22.56 – Hamburg Hbf 23.07 – HH Dammtor 23.13 – **Hamburg-Altona 23.21**	10 a/b
⑤ 20.27	IC 1632	*Seemöwe* Bochum 20.39 – Essen 20.50 – Duisburg 21.03 – Düsseldorf 21.18 – **Köln 21.42**	16 a/b
⑦ 20.27 auch 17. VI., nicht 16. VI.	D 1838	Bochum 20.39 – Essen 20.50 – Duisburg 21.03 – Düsseldorf 21.18 – **Köln 21.44**	16 a/b
20.29 außer ⑥	6192 2.	DO Westfalenhalle 20.34 – DO Tierpark 20.37 – Herdecke 20.51 – Hagen 21.01 – Brügge 21.46 – **Lüdenscheid 21.57**	6
✗ 20.31 außer ⑥	5283	Kamen 20.46 – **Hamm 20.58**	8 a/b
† 20.32	7145	Lünen 20.48 – Werne 20.57 – **Münster 21.36**	11 a/b
20.33	5681	DO Westfalenhalle 20.38 – DO-Hörde 20.42 – Holzwickede 20.53 – **Unna 20.58**	3
20.35	IC 632	*Graf Luckner* Bochum 20.47 – Essen 20.58 – Duisburg 21.11 – Düsseldorf 21.26 – **Köln 21.50**	16 a/b
⑦ 20.37 auch 17. VI., nicht 16. VI.	D 1733 2.	Hamm 20.54 – Münster 21.16 – Osnabrück 21.45 – Bremen 22.48 – HH-Harburg 24.00 – Hamburg Hbf 0.16 – Neumünster 1.19 – **Flensburg 2.32**	10 a/b
⑦ 20.42 auch 17. VI., nicht 16. VI.	D 1743	Bielefeld 21.38 – Herford 21.48 – Hannover 22.58 – Hildesheim 23.25 – Kreiensen 23.59 – Northeim 0.12 – **Göttingen 0.26**	8 a/b
† 20.42	7649	Lünen 20.52 – Lüdinghausen 21.12 – Dülmen 21.21 – **Coesfeld 21.47** *Ohne Halt bis Lünen*	21 a/b

A Listen carefully to the recording of people buying train tickets and find out which of the tickets below is being bought in each case.

a

DB	Erster Geltungstag	Zur Hinfahrt	Zur Rückfahrt gültig bis einschließlich	Ausgabe-Nr
	13.04.			132972

Klasse	Tarif	halber Preis
XX	IC-ZUSCHLAG************	KIND

von   RES O

nach
über

Verkaufsstelle	Z A	km	DM
WUPPERTAL-ELBERFELD	XX	0000	****2.50
	0014****		222

Bitte Rückseite beachten

b

DB	Erster Geltungstag	Zur Hinfahrt	Zur Rückfahrt gültig bis einschließlich	Ausgabe-Nr
	14.08.	13.10.	13.10.	006414

Klasse	Tarif	halber Preis
2	MINIGR 3 P -H+R-******	--- --- --- ---

von   BULLAY (DB)   E/K:02/02

nach TRIER
über WENGEROHR
709   663

Verkaufsstelle	Z A	km	DM
BULLAY (DB)	XX	0054	****44.00
	25110851		

Bitte Rückseite beachten

c

DB	Erster Geltungstag	Zur Hinfahrt	Zur Rückfahrt gültig bis einschließlich	Ausgabe-Nr
	15.12.	18.12.	--- --- ---	475905

Klasse	Tarif	Halb Preis
2	EINFACHE FAHRT********	--- --- --- ---

von   NUERNBERG

nach SCHWAEBISCH HALL
über CR*SCHWAEB.HALL-HESSENT

Verkaufsstelle	Z A	km	DM
22194553	XX	0126	***21,00

NUERNBERG HBF   *RFE*

d

DB **Tramper-Monats-Ticket**

Gültig vom **17.03.1989**
bis **16.04.1989**

A

Nr 528941

2. Klasse

238,00 DM
Steuersatz 14%

(Eigenhändige Unterschrift des Inhabers, Vor- und Familienname mit Tinte oder Kugelschreiber ausgeschrieben.)

B Listen to the recording again. Copy the following grid into your notebook and complete it:

	Destination	Price	No. of people	Type of ticket	Any other info.
1					
2					
3					
4					

Jetzt bist du dran!

Work with a partner. Take the roles of customer and clerk at the ticket office, and ask each other for the tickets as indicated on the cue cards below:

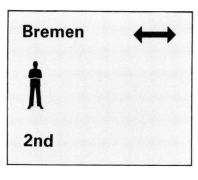

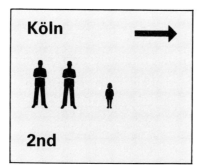

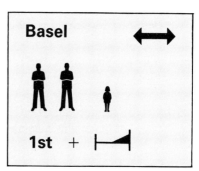

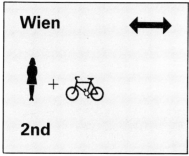

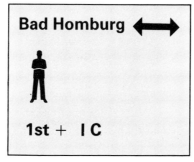

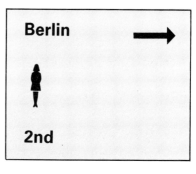

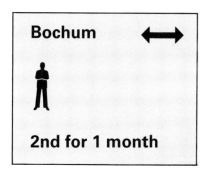

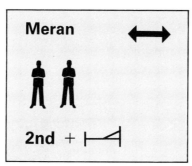

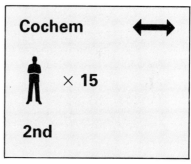

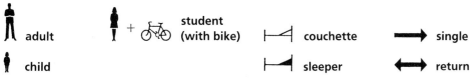

B. In der Stadt

Hör zu! ❻

A Listen to the following conversations, in which directions are asked for and given. Turn to worksheet A of this unit. For each conversation, fill in the destination and the directions given.

B Listen to the recordings again. For each conversation, note down on the worksheet the German expressions for the phrases given on tape.

Jetzt bist du dran! 💬

Work through the following situations with your partner, asking for and receiving directions to a particular destination. Once you have been through all the situations once, change roles.

You ask, for example: Entschuldigen Sie bitte. Wie komme ich am besten zum Adelphi-Kino?

Your partner replies: Sie fahren am besten mit der Straßenbahn, Linie 6, bis zur Bismarckstraße. Da steigen Sie um in den Bus, Linie 83, bis nach Horstbrunnen. Das Kino ist in der Nähe der Haltestelle. Die Fahrt dauert ungefähr 15 Minuten.

	1	2	3
You want to go to:	Adelphi-Kino	Krankenhaus	Adam-Kraft-Gymnasium
Take the:	tram line 6	underground	S-Bahn, number 6
to:	Bismarckstraße	zoo	main station
From there take:	bus, line 83	bus, line 92	bus no. 23
Get off at:	Horstbrunnen	Lukasplatz	Adam-Kraft-Straße
This will take you:	15 minutes	10 minutes	20 minutes

	4	5
You want to go to:	Universität	Kunstgalerie
Take the:	tram, line 13	tram, line 3
to:	Wittenbergplatz	Rathaus
From there take:	underground, line 1	S-Bahn 9
Get off at:	Ernst-Reuter-Platz	Dürerstraße
This will take you:	10–15 minutes	half an hour

Entwerten 📖

Read this notice and fill in the blanks in the passage below.

Entwertung der Fahrausweise durch den Fahrgast

Zu entwerten sind alle Fahrausweise mit dem Hinweis „Nur gültig mit Entwerteraufdruck".

Das sind Einzel-, Mehrfahrten-, 24-Stunden- und Gruppen-fahrausweise. Ohne Entwertung sind die Fahrausweise nicht gültig.

Bitte stempeln Sie Ihren Fahrausweis bei **Fahrtantritt** in den **orangefarbenen** Entwertern ab. Diese befinden sich

○ auf den mit 🚃, Ⓢ, Ⓤ oder 🚈 gekennzeichneten **Bahnhöfen**
○ in Straßenbahnen und Bussen **im Fahrzeug**.

Fahrausweise aus Fahrausweisdruckern in Bussen und Straßen-bahnen sind in der Regel bereits entwertet.

Überzeugen Sie sich bitte, daß Ihr Fahrausweis einen Entwerteraufdruck trägt.

Wenn Sie mit einer Wochen- oder Monatskarte fahren, tragen Sie bitte vor der ersten Fahrt die Nummer Ihrer Kundenkarte in die Wertmarke ein.

Kapiert?

If your ticket has not been . . . , it is not . . . . your ticket before your journey . . .! The machines are . . . in colour. If you have a weekly or a . . . ticket, make sure that you fill in the . . . of your customer card before your . . . journey.

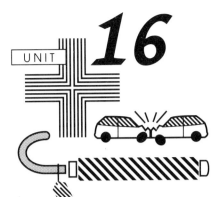
In this unit you will practise:

▷ describing and enquiring about items lost,

▶ how to get help when you need it,

▷ how to report an accident,

▶ how to make an appointment for and consult medical help,

▷ how to purchase medicine.

A. Verloren – Gefunden

Hör zu! ❶

You will hear some recordings of people reporting the loss of some of their belongings. Listen carefully to the descriptions they give, and write down the following information in your notebook:

a) the item that has been lost,

b) a detailed description of it,

c) the circumstances under which it was lost.

Jetzt bist du dran!

You have gone to the *Fundbüro* (lost property office), because you have lost something. The attendant (your partner will take this role) asks you for a detailed description of the object. Tell him/her what the item looks like, using the vocabulary below as well as our example on the next page to help you.

Es ist aus	Leder	(gemacht/gefertigt).
	Plastik	
	Holz	
	Wolle	
	Baumwolle	
	Glas	
	Gummi	
	Kunststoff	
	Metall	
	Nylon	
	Stoff	
	Gold	
	Silber	
	Messing	

Der Artikel ist	rot	neu	japanisch
	grün	alt	englisch
	weiß	lang	deutsch
	schwarz	kurz	amerikanisch
	gelb	groß	italienisch
	grau	klein	spanisch
	braun	rund	
	blau	schmal	
	dunkel-. . .	breit	
	hell-. . .	viereckig	
	orange	kariert	
		gestreift	
		gepunkt	
Mein Name	steht	(nicht)	darauf.
	ist		eingraviert.

The conversation might be conducted on the following lines:

You: Guten Tag. Ich habe meine Handtasche im Bus liegenlassen. Hat man sie vielleicht hier abgegeben?

Attendant: Wie sieht sie denn aus?

You: Sie ist aus Leder. Sie ist grau und ziemlich klein. Leider steht mein Name nicht darauf. Sie hat einen großen Metallverschluß.

B. Panne

Notruf

Your car has just broken down, and you see this emergency telephone. How do you operate it? Explain to your teacher in German.

Hör zu! ❷

Listen to the telephone conversation from an emergency phone on a motorway. Write down:

a) what has happened,
b) what sort of a car it is,
c) its registration number,

d) its colour,
e) how long the person will have to wait.

Jetzt bist du dran!

Imagine your car has broken down on the motorway. Your partner plays the part of the *Autobahnmeisterei*. Supply the appropriate information.

Your partner: Autobahnmeisterei.
You: Say hello, and then say what is wrong.
Your partner: Was haben Sie für einen Wagen?

You: Say what sort of car you have.
Your partner: Kennzeichen?
You: Give the registration number.
Your partner: Farbe?
You: Say what colour it is.
Your partner: In 20 Minuten wird ein Wagen bei Ihnen sein.
You: Thank him very much.

C. Ein Unfall

Hör zu! ❸

You are spending an afternoon on duty with your penfriend's mother, who works in a police station. She receives the following accident reports over the phone. You listen in on an extension and note down the following information from each report:

a) a description of the location of the accident,

b) the number of people involved,

c) whether people were injured and if so, how many,

d) the name and address of the person who rang.

Jetzt bist du dran!

Act out the following situation with your partner, with one of you reporting an accident to the police (the partner). Change roles when you have gone through a situation once.

Your partner: Hier Polizeiwache am Hauptbahnhof.
You: Give your name; say you want to report an accident.
Your partner: Wo ist der Unfall passiert?
You: a) at the crossroads Hauptstraße and Turnstraße.
                b) in the Baumschulallee.
                c) at the junction Arndtstraße and Goethestraße.
Your partner: Wer war an dem Unfall beteiligt?
You: a) a lorry and a bus.
                b) a motorcyclist and a VW.
                c) an Opel and a Mercedes.
Your partner: Gibt es Verletzte?
You: a) Yes, the driver of the bus and some passengers.
                b) The motorcyclist is seriously injured. The driver of
                   the VW slightly.
                c) The driver of the Opel is slightly injured. The driver
                   of the Mercedes not at all.

Here are some expressions to help you:

Hier ist ein Unfall passiert/geschehen.

An der Kreuzung . . .-straße und . . .-straße/an der Ecke . . .-straße und
. . .-straße/in der . . .-straße.

. . . Personen sind leicht/schwer verletzt.

Es gibt . . . Verletzte/keine Verletzen.

D. Beim Arzt

Look at the doctor's notices below.
Find the right doctor for each of the following people:

a) Someone who is hard of hearing.
b) Someone with poor eyesight.
c) Someone with toothache.
d) A sick baby.
e) Someone with the flu.

1.

2.

4.

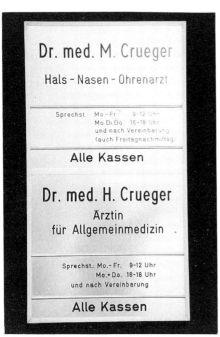

3.

5.

Hör zu! ❹

A You will hear eight short recordings, in which some ailments and injuries are mentioned. Listen carefully. Whenever your teacher stops the tape, write down what the problem is.

B Look at worksheet A of this unit. Write the German names of the injuries or ailments mentioned into the relevant place(s) in the drawing.

Hör zu! ❺

Your penfriend's sister has invited you to spend an afternoon with her in the reception of the doctor's surgery where she works. She allows you to listen in on the telephone conversations with patients who make appointments. Listen carefully, and write down as much information as you can gather on the following points:

a) the reason why the patient wants to see the doctor,

b) for how long the patient has suffered from the complaint,

c) when the appointment is being made for.

Jetzt bist du dran!

You feel unwell and wish to see a doctor. Ring the surgery (your partner) and make an appointment. Make sure you give the following information:

a) your name,
b) your illness/complaint,
c) how long you have suffered from it,
d) suggest a date for an appointment.

So kannst du es sagen

Here is some vocabulary to help you with your conversation:

a) **Problem**:

Ich habe	Bauchschmerzen
	Halsschmerzen
	Kopfschmerzen
	Rückenschmerzen
	eine Verletzung
	  am Bein, Arm, Kopf,
	  Knie, etc.
		einen Sonnenbrand
		einen Schnupfen
		eine Erkältung
		die Grippe
		die Windpocken/die Masern/Mums
		Durchfall

Ich bin von einer Wespe gestochen worden.

Ich habe mir	die Hand verletzt. den Arm gebrochen. das Bein verstaucht. die Hand verbrannt. den Kopf aufgeschlagen.

b) **Seit**:

> gestern
> vorgestern
> letzte Woche
> fünf Tagen
> heute morgen

c) **Termin**:

> Morgen früh, um . . . Uhr.
> Morgen nachmittag, um . . .
>   Uhr.
> Übermorgen.
> Nächste Woche.
> Montag, den . . . -ten um . . .
>   Uhr.

Hör zu! ❻

Listen to the following three conversations in a doctor's treatment room. When your teacher stops the tape, note down the following information in your notebook about each conversation:

a) the patient's complaint,

b) the doctor's diagnosis,

c) the doctor's advice and/or treatment.

Hör zu! ❼

You will hear some conversations at a chemist's. Listen carefully, and take notes on the following points in your notebook:

a) what the customer asks for,

b) what he/she buys,

c) how and when the medication is to be taken,

d) how much it costs.